Sefer

Messilat Yesharim

מסילת ישרים

לרמח"ל

Kabbalist Rabbi

Moshe Chaim Luzzatto

The Ra'MHaL

There is no known book without mistakes. Therefore, I ask in every language of application if anyone has any questions, comments, clarifications, corrections, please send to: **book@simchatchaim.com**

All material used in this section may not be used for commercial purposes, but only for study and teaching.

To get this book or books and information Email me at:

book@simchatchaim.com

Copyright©All Rights Reserved to

www.simchatchaim.com

YB"S©All rights reserved to the Editor

First Edition 2023

TABLE OF CONTENTS

Page	Contents
3	The Ra'Mhal
9	Introduction
19	Chapter 1
29	Chapter 2
33	Chapter 3
41	Chapter 4
55	Chapter 5
63	Chapter 6
71	Chapter 7
77	Chapter 8
81	Chapter 9
89	Chapter 10
95	Chapter 11

141	Chapter 12	
143	Chapter 13	
153	Chapter 14	
157	Chapter 15	
161	Chapter 16	
167	Chapter 17	
171	Chapter 18	
175	Chapter 19	
209	Chapter 20	
217	Chapter 21	
221	Chapter 22	
235	Chapter 23	
243	Chapter 24	
251	Chapter 25	
255	Chapter 26	

Moshe Chaim Luzzatto

Moshe Chaim Luzzatto (Ra'Mhal) was an Italian rabbi, kabbalist and philosopher who also wrote dramatic works and literary criticism. Gifted with an almost photographic memory, he wrote many works, some which became standards of kabbalah and ethics. He was suspected of Sabbateanism, but was exonerated by his teachers and colleagues with a warning to cease engaging in speculative Kabbalistic writing. Toward the end of his life he moved to the Land of Israel.

Early life

Moshe Chaim Luzzatto was born in 1707 in the Jewish Ghetto of Padua, Italy. The son of Jacob Vita and Diamente Luzzatto, he received classical Jewish and Italian education, showing a predilection for literature at a very early age. He may have attended the University of Padua and certainly associated with a group of students there, known to dabble in mysticism and alchemy. With his vast knowledge in religious lore, the arts, and science, he quickly became the dominant figure in that group. His writings demonstrate mastery of the Tanakh, the Talmud, and the rabbinical commentaries and codes of Jewish law.

Poetry and literature

At an early age, he began a thorough study of the Hebrew language and of poetic composition. He wrote epithalamia and elegies, a noteworthy example of the latter being the dirge on the death of his teacher Cantarini, a lofty poem of twenty-four verses written in classical Hebrew. Before age 20, he had begun his composition of

150 hymns modeled on the Biblical Psalter. In these psalms, composed in conformity with the laws of parallelism, he freed himself from all foreign influences, imitating the style of the Bible so faithfully that his poems seem entirely a renaissance of Biblical words and thoughts. They provoked the criticism of the Rabbis, however, and were one of the causes of the persecutions to which Luzzatto was later subjected. R. Jacob Poppers of Frankfort-on-the-Main thought it unpardonable presumption to attempt to equal the "anointed of the God of Jacob." Only two psalms are known of which it can with certainty be said that they belonged to Luzzatto's psalter; in addition seven hymns by him which were sung at the inauguration of the enlarged Spanish synagogue at Padua appeared in the work "Hanukkat ha-Maron" (Venice, 1729); but it is not certain whether they were taken from the psalter.

As a youth Luzzatto essayed also dramatic poetry, writing at the age of 17 his first Biblical drama, "Shimshon U-Felistim," (of which only fragments have been preserved, in another work of his). This youthful production foreshadows the coming master; it is perfect in versification, simple in language, original and thoughtful in substance. This first large work was followed by the "Leshon Limmudim," a discussion of Hebrew style with a new theory of Hebrew versification, in which the author showed his thorough knowledge of classical rhetoric. It is in a certain sense a scientific demonstration of the neoclassic Italian style, in contrast with the medieval. There is a vast difference between Luzzatto style, which recalls the simplicity, smoothness, and vigor of the Bible, and the insipid, exaggerated, and affected work of his contemporaries. The book, dedicated to his teacher Bassani, was printed at Mantua 1727, with a text which deviates from the manuscript formerly in the possession of M. S. Ghirondi.

In the same year or somewhat later, Luzzatto wrote his allegorical festival drama "Migdal 'Oz" (or "Tummat Yesharim"), on the occasion of the marriage of his friend Israel Benjamin Bassani. This four-act play, which shows Latin and Italian as well as Biblical influence, illustrates the victory of justice over iniquity. It is masterly in versification and melodious in language, the lyrical passages being especially lofty; and it has a wealth of pleasing imagery reminiscent of Guarini's "Pastor Fido." The drama was edited by M. Letteris, and published with notes by S. D. Luzzatto and prolegomena by Franz Delitzsch, Leipsic, 1837.

Controversy
The turning point in Luzzatto life came at the age of twenty, when he claimed to have received direct instruction from an angel (known as a maggid). While stories of such encounters with celestial entities were not unknown in kabbalistic circles, it was unheard of for someone of such a young age. His peers were enthralled by his written accounts of these "Divine lessons", but the leading Italian rabbinical authorities were highly suspicious and threatened to excommunicate him. Just one hundred years earlier another young mystic, Shabbatai Zvi (1626–1676), had rocked the Jewish world by claiming to be the Messiah. Although, at one point,

Zvi had convinced many European and Middle Eastern rabbis of his claim, the episode ended with him recanting and converting to Islam. The global Jewish community was still reeling from that, and the similarities between Luzzatto writings and Zvi's were perceived as being particularly dangerous and heretical.

These writings, only some of which have survived, are often misunderstood to describe a belief that the Ramchal and his followers were key figures in a messianic drama that was about to take place. In this contentious interpretation, he identified one of his followers as the Messiah, son of David, and assumed for himself the role of Moses, claiming that he was that biblical figure's reincarnation.

Departure from Italy

After threats of excommunication and many arguments, Luzzatto finally came to an understanding with the leading Italian rabbis, including his decision not to write the maggid's lessons or teach mysticism. In 1735, Luzzatto left Italy for Amsterdam, believing that in the more liberal environment there, he would be able to pursue his mystical interests. Passing through Germany, he appealed to the local rabbinical authorities to protect him from the threats of the Italian rabbis. They refused and forced him to sign a document stating that all the teachings of the maggid were false.

Amsterdam

When Luzzatto finally reached Amsterdam, he was able to pursue his Kabbalah studies relatively unhindered. Earning a living as a diamond cutter, he continued writing but refused to teach. It was in this period that he wrote his magnum opus the Mesillat Yesharim (1740), essentially an ethical treatise but with certain mystical underpinnings. The book presents a step-by-step process by which every person can overcome the inclination to sin and might eventually experience a divine inspiration similar to prophecy. Another prominent work, Derekh Hashem (The Way of God) is a concise work on the core theology of Judaism. The same concepts are discussed in brief in a smaller book called Maamar HaIkarim (the English translation of this book is now available on the Web with the title "Essay on Fundamentals"). Da'at Tevunot ("The Knowing Heart") also found its existence in Amsterdam as the missing link between rationality and Kabbalah, a dialogue between the intellect and the soul. On the other hand, Derech Tevunot ("The Way of Understanding") introduces the logic which structures Talmudic debates as a means to understanding the world. One major rabbinic contemporary who praised Luzzatto writing was Rabbi Eliyahu of Vilna, the Vilna Gaon (1720–1797), who was considered to be the most authoritative Torah sage of the modern era as well as a great kabbalist himself. He was reputed to have said after reading the Mesillat Yesharim, that were Luzzatto still alive, he would have walked from Vilna to learn at Luzzatto feet. He stated that having read the work, the first ten chapters contained not a superfluous word.

Luzzatto also wrote poetry and drama. Although most of it is seemingly secular, some scholars claim to have identified mystical undertones in this body of work as well. His writing is strongly influenced by the Jewish poets of Spain and by contemporary Italian authors.

The cantor of the Sephardic synagogue in Amsterdam, Abraham Caceres, worked with Luzzatto to set several of his poems to music.

Acre, Israel
Frustrated by his inability to teach kabbalah, Luzzatto left Amsterdam for the Holy Land in 1743, settling in Acre. Three years later, he and his family died in a plague.

Legacy
Though it is accepted by scholars that his tomb is in Kafr Yasif, where some assume to have identified it, his burial place is traditionally said to be near the Talmudic sage Rabbi Akiva in Tiberias, northern Israel. It is noteworthy that there are many scholars who make some comparison between the Ramchal and Rabbi Akiva. Some believe that the Ramchal is actually a Gilgul (reincarnation) of Rabbi Akiva. Probably also because Kafr Yasif is now an Arab town while Tiberias is Jewish, the Tiberias tomb is the destination of almost all of the pilgrims seeking his final resting place.

Messilat Yesharim

Introduction

The writer says: I have composed this work not to teach people what they do not know but to remind them of what they already know and which is very familiar to them. For you will find in most of my words only things which most people already know and do not have any doubt about.

But according to their familiarity and to the extent that their truth is evident to all, so too is their neglect very prevalent and forgetfulness of them very great. Therefore, the benefit to be gleaned from this book is not from a single reading, for it is possible that the reader will learn little that he did not already know. Rather the benefit derived [from this book] comes from review and diligent study. For [then] he will be reminded of these things which, by nature, people tend to forget and he will put to heart his duties which he hides from.

If you reflect on the current state of affairs in most of the world, you will see most people of quick intelligence and sharp mentality devote most of their thought and interest in the subtleties of wisdom and the depths of analysis; every man according to his intellectual tendency and natural desire.

There are those who toil greatly in studying the creation and nature. Others devote all their study to astronomy and mathematics, or to the arts. There are others which enter closer towards the sacred, namely, the study of the holy Torah. Among those, some occupy themselves with Halachic analyses, others with Midrash, others with law decisions.

But few are those which devote thought and study to the matter of perfection of [divine] service: on love, fear, clinging, and the other branches of piety. This is not because they do not consider these things as fundamental. For if you ask them, each one will answer you that this is of utmost importance and that it is unimaginable for one to be considered truly wise if he has not fully comprehended these matters.

Rather their lack of devoting more attention to it stems from its being so familiar and so evident to them that they see no need for spending much time on it.

[Consequently] this study and the reading of books of this sort is left to people of not so keen, almost dull intelligence.

These types of people you will find diligent in all this, not budging from it, until the situation has reached the point that if one sees a person engaging in piety, he cannot help but suspecting him of belonging to those of dull intelligence.

The consequences of this situation are very evil both for those who possess wisdom and those who do not. For it causes both types to lack true piety thereby making it exceedingly rare to be found anywhere in the world.

It is absent from the wise due to their insufficient reflection on it, and likewise to the non-wise due to their insufficient grasp of it.

The situation has reached the point where most people imagine piety consists of reciting many psalms, very long confessions, difficult fasts, and immersions in ice [water] and snow - all are things incompatible with intellect and which reason cannot find peace.

Thus, the true piety that is acceptable and cherished is far from what our minds conceive to us. For it is obvious "that which a person does not feel a responsibility to do, does not occupy a place on his mind".

Although the beginnings and foundations of [piety] are already implanted in every upright person's heart, nevertheless if he does not engage himself in their study, he will encounter its branches but won't recognize them and he will tread over them without perceiving that he is doing so.

Observe that matters of piety and fear and love [of G-d], and purity of heart are not things innately implanted in a person whereby he would not need means to acquire them such as sleep and wakefulness, hunger and satiation, and all the other responses naturally implanted in our nature. Rather, certainly it is necessary to employ means and strategies to acquire them.

There is also no lack of detrimental factors which distance a person from them, but correspondingly there is also no lack of ways by which these obstacles may be held afar.

If so, then how can one not need to devote time on this study - to know the truth of these matters, and learn the means to acquire them and fulfill them? From where will this wisdom come in the heart of a person if he does not seek it?!

Since it is clear to every wise man the need for perfection of the divine service, and the necessity for its purity and cleanliness, for without this it is certainly not acceptable at all, but rather it is repulsive and despised since "the L-rd searches all hearts, and discerns all the imaginations of the thoughts [if you seek Him, He will be found of you; but if you forsake Him, He will cast you off for ever]" (I Chronicles 28:9).

What will we answer on the day of rebuke if we have been lax in this study, and forsaken that which is so incumbent on us as to be the main thing which the L-rd our G-d requires of us?

Is it conceivable for us to exert our minds and labor in logical inquiries which we are not obligated in, in sharp discourses bearing no fruit, and laws which are not relevant to us - and that which is so great a debt to our Creator, we abandon it to habit and surrender it to rote practice?!

If we do not look into and analyze what is true fear of G-d and what are its branches, how can we ever acquire it? And how can we ever save ourselves from the worldly vanities which causes our heart to be forgetful of it?! Will it not be forgotten and go away even though we recognize its necessity!

Likewise, for love of G-d - if we do not exert ourselves to implant it in our heart through all the means which lead to this, how will it exist within us?!

From where will come the cleaving, and the passion in our souls to the blessed G-d and His Torah if we don't give attention to His greatness and exaltedness which instills in our hearts this cleaving?

How will we purify our thoughts if we don't exert ourselves to cleanse it from the imperfections instilled in them by physical nature?! And what of all our character traits, who likewise are in need of so much rectification and correction. Who will correct them and who will rectify them if we do not attend to them and are not exceedingly meticulous in this?!

If we truly examined the matter, we would discover the truth of this thereby benefiting ourselves and teaching it to others to benefit them also. This is what Shlomo said: "If you will seek it as silver and search for it as buried treasure, then you will understand the fear of G-d" (Mishlei 2:4-5).

He didn't say "then you will understand philosophy; then you will understand astronomy; then you will understand medicine; then you will understand legal decisions; then you will understand laws" - but rather "then you will understand fear of G-d"! Behold from here, that to understand the fear of G-d one must seek it like silver and search for it like buried treasure. Is it sufficient then what we have been taught by our forefathers and what is familiar to every observant person in a general sense?

Is it conceivable that we find time for all other branches of study but not for this study?

Why shouldn't a man set aside for himself, at least, fixed times for this study if he is forced, for the rest of his time, to turn to other studies or affairs?

Behold scripture says: "Hen fear of G-d - this is wisdom" (Job 28:28). Our Sages of blessed memory commented (Shab 31b), "'Hen' [hints to] 'one', for in Greek 'one' is designated as 'Hen'". Behold, that fear of G-d is considered wisdom - and this alone is [true] wisdom. And certainly, that which does not require investigation cannot be called "wisdom".

In truth, a great amount of analysis is needed in all of these things if they are to be known in truth, not as imagination and deluded logic. How much more so to acquire them and attain them.

He who contemplates into these matters will see that piety does not depend on those things which the foolishly pious think but rather on true perfection and great wisdom.

This is what Moshe, our teacher, peace be unto him, teaches us saying: "And now, Israel, what does the L-rd your G-d ask of you, but that you fear the L-rd your G-d to walk in all His ways, and to love Him and serve the L-rd your G-d with all your heart and all your soul, to keep the mitzvot (commandments) of G-d and His statutes..." (Deut. 10:12)

Here he encompassed all the divisions of perfection of divine service that is desirable to the blessed G-d. They are: fear [of G-d], walking in His ways, love [of G-d], wholeheartedness, and observance of all of the commandments.

Fear [of G-d] - this is fear of the exaltedness of G-d, namely, that one fears before Him like he would fear before a great and awesome king, feeling abashed by His greatness before making any movement before Him. All the more so, when speaking before Him in prayer or studying His Torah.

Walking in His ways - this includes all matters of uprightness and correction of character traits. This is what our sages of blessed memory explained (Shab.133b) "just as He is merciful, be also merciful..." The general principle of all this is for one to conduct all of his traits in all the variety of his deeds according to what is just and ethical.

Our sages of blessed memory summarized this saying: "[what is the proper path a person should choose for himself?] Whatever is harmonious for the one who does it, and harmonious for other people" (Pirkei Avot 2:1). That is, that which leads to the goal of true beneficence, namely, strengthening of Torah and furthering of societal brotherliness.

Love - that one has implanted in his heart love of G-d, until his soul is moved to do what is pleasing to Him just like his heart is moved to do what is pleasing to his father and mother. He will be pained if he or others are lacking in this. He will be zealous for it and feels great joy in doing something of this.

Wholeheartedness - that service before the blessed G-d be with purity of motive, namely, for the sake of His service alone and not for any other motive.

This also includes that one be wholeheartedly devoted in his service, and not like one "wavering between two sides" (Kings 18:21), or like one doing out of habitual rote. Rather, that his whole heart be devoted to this.

Observing all of the commandments - as the words indicate, namely, to observe all of the commandments in their entirety, in all their detailed rules and conditions.

Behold, all of these general principles require a lengthy explanation. I have found that our sages of blessed memory have encompassed all of these divisions [of divine service] in different words arranged according to the order of steps needed to properly acquire them. It was taught in a Beraitha and cited in several places in the Talmud. One of these is in the chapter "before their festivals" (Avodah Zara 20b): ["you shall guard yourself from everything evil" - Devarim 23:10...]

"From here Rabbi Pinchas ben Yair derived:

Torah brings to watchfulness;

Watchfulness brings to Zeal;

Zeal brings to Cleanliness;

Cleanliness brings to Separation;

Separation brings to Purity;

Purity brings to Piety;

Piety brings to Humility;

Humility brings to Fear of Sin;

Fear of Sin brings to Holiness;

Holiness brings to the Holy Spirit,

and the Holy Spirit brings to the Revival of the Dead."

On the basis of this beraitha I have undertaken to compose this work; to teach myself and to remind others the conditions of perfect service according to their proper levels. I will clarify the nature of each one of them, its divisions and details, the way to acquire it, its detrimental factors and the way to guard against them so that I and whoever else finds it pleasing may read it in order to learn to fear the L-rd our G-d, and not forget our duty to Him. What the natural physicality exerts itself to remove from our hearts, the reading and reflecting will remind us and awaken us to that which we have been commanded.

May G-d be our trust and keep our feet from stumbling (Prov.3:26), and may there be fulfilled in us the request of the Psalmist, beloved of his G-d, "Teach me your ways, O G-d; I shall walk in your truth: make one my heart to fear Your Name"(Ps. 86:11).

Messilat Yesharim

Chapter 1

The foundation of piety and the root of perfect service [of G-d] is for a man to clarify and come to realize as truth what is his obligation in his world and to what he needs to direct his gaze and his aspiration in all that he toils all the days of his life.

Behold, what our sages, of blessed memory, have taught us is that man was created solely to delight in G-d and to derive pleasure in the radiance of the Shechina (divine presence). For this is the true delight and the greatest pleasure that can possibly exist. The place of this pleasure is, in truth, in Olam Haba (the World to Come). For it was created expressly for this purpose.

But the path to arrive at the "desired haven" (Ps. 107:30) of ours is this world. This is what our sages of blessed memory said: "this world is like a corridor before the World to Come" (Avot 4:16).

The means that lead a person to this goal are the commandments which the blessed G-d commanded to us. The place of the performance of these commandments is only in this world. Therefore, man was first placed in this world so that through these means prepared for him here, he will be able to reach the place prepared for him, namely, the World to Come, there to be sated with the good which he acquired through these means. This is what our sages of blessed memory said "today to do them, and tomorrow to receive their reward" (Eruvin 22:1).

When you look further into the matter, you will see that true perfection lies only in clinging to G-d. This is what King David said "But as for me, closeness to G-d is my good" (Ps. 73:28) and, "one thing I asked from G-d; that I seek, that I may dwell in G-d's house all the days of my life, to gaze on the pleasantness of G-d..." (Ps. 27:4). For only this is the good, while anything besides this that people consider good is really emptiness and mistaken worthlessness.

For a person to attain this good, it is proper that he first exert himself strenuously to acquire it, namely, to exert himself to cling to the blessed G-d through the power of deeds whose consequence is this end. These deeds are the commandments.

The Holy One, blessed be He, has put man in a place where the factors which distance him from the blessed G-d are numerous. These are the physical lusts which if he is drawn after them, behold, he draws away and goes ever further from the true good.

Thus, we see that man is truly placed in the midst of a raging battlefield. For all matters of this world, whether for the good or for the bad, are trials for a man. Poverty from one side versus wealth from the other. This is as Shlomo said: "Lest I be satiated, and deny You, and say, Who is G-d? or lest I be poor, and steal..." (Prov.30:9). Tranquility on one hand versus suffering on the other, until the battle is waged against him from the front and from the rear.

If he will be a man of valor, emerging from the battle victorious on all fronts - he will be the "Adam HaShalem" (whole/perfect man) who will merit to cling to his Creator and will emerge from this corridor to enter into the palace to enlighten in the Light of (eternal) Life.

According to the extent that he conquered his inclination and lusts, and distanced from the factors which distance him from the good, and exerted himself to cling to G-d, to that extent will he attain it and rejoice in it.

If you look deeper into the matter, you will see that this world was created for man's use. But, behold man stands on a great balance. For if he is drawn after the world and distances from his Creator, behold, he corrupts himself and corrupts the world with him. But if he rules over himself and clings to his Creator, and uses the world only as an aid to serve his Creator - then he elevates himself and elevates the world with him. For all creations are greatly elevated when they serve the "Adam HaShalem" (whole/perfect man) who is sanctified with the holiness of the blessed G-d.

This is like what our sages of blessed memory said regarding the light which G-d stored away for the righteous (Chagiga 12a): "when G-d saw the light which He stored away for the righteous, He rejoiced, as written: 'the light of the righteous rejoices' (Prov.13:9)".

And regarding the "stones of the place" which Yaakov took and placed under his head the Midrash says (Chulin 91b): "Rabbi Yitzchak says: 'this teaches us that they gathered together in one place, each one saying: let the righteous man lay his head upon me'".

Our sages roused us to this fundamental principle in Midrash Kohelet saying: "see the work of G-d." (Ecc. 7:13), "when the Holy One, Blessed be He, created Adam, He took him and led him to pass before all the trees of the Garden of Eden and said to him: 'see how beautiful and excellent are my works. All that I have created, I have created for your sake. Be careful that you do not become corrupt and destroy My world.'"

The general principle of this matter: man was not created for his state in this world, but rather, for his state in the World to Come. Only that his state in this world is a means towards his state in the World to Come, which is his ultimate purpose.

Hence, you will find many statements of our sages, of blessed memory, all along similar lines, comparing this world to a place and time of preparation while the next world is compared to a place of rest and eating what has already been prepared. For instance they said: "this world is like a corridor" (Avos 4:16), as I wrote earlier; "today for their performance and tomorrow [for receiving their reward]..." (Avodah Zara 3a); "He who toiled on Friday will eat on the Sabbath" (Kohelet Raba 1:15); "this world is like the shore and the next world like the sea", and many other statements along the same lines.

Indeed, you can see that no rational person can possibly believe that the purpose of man's creation is for his existence in this world. For what is man's life in this world? Who is truly happy and content in this world? "The days of our life are 70 years, and if by strength, 80 years, yet their span is but toil and trouble" (Ps. 90:10).

How many sorts of distress and sicknesses, pain and burdens, and after all that death! Not one in a thousand can be found to whom this world has granted plenty of pleasures and true contentment. And even such a person, if he reaches the age of a hundred years, already [is as one who already] passed and disappeared from the world.

Furthermore, if the purpose of man's creation were for the sake of this world, it would not have been necessary to imbue him with such a lofty and exalted soul, greater even than the angels themselves.

Especially so, when the soul finds no satisfaction whatsoever from all the pleasures of this world. This is what our sages teach us in Midrash Kohelet: "'but the soul will not be fulfilled' (Kohelet 6:7) - What is this analogous to? To the case of a common peasant who married the king's daughter. Even if he brought her all that the village possessed, it would be as nothing to her. For she is the king's daughter. So too with the soul, if you would bring to her all the pleasures of this world, they would be like nothing to her. For she is from higher worlds" (Kohelet Raba 6:7).

Likewise, our sages of blessed memory taught us: "against your will you were formed, and against your will you were born" (Avot 4:22). For the soul does not love this world at all. On the contrary, it despises it. If so, certainly, the Creator, blessed be His Name, would never have created something for a purpose which is against its nature and despised by it!

Rather, man's creation was for his state in the world to come. Therefore, this soul was placed in him, for it befits the soul to serve G-d; and through it a man will be rewarded in proper time and place. Thus, this world will not be something despised to his soul, but rather beloved and cherished by it. This is evident.

Behold, after knowing all this, we will immediately realize the grave obligation of the commandments upon us and the preciousness of the Divine service which lies in our hands. For these are the means which lead us to the true perfection. Without them, this state will not be attained in the least.

It is known that a purpose is not attained without the combined contribution of all the means found and employed to achieve it. According to the capacity of the means and their use will be the resulting achievement of purpose and any slight deviation found in the employed means will be very noticeable in the end result derived from their combined contributions. This is self-evident.

It is obvious therefore, that we must be meticulous to the utmost degree in the manner of observance of the commandments and the service of G-d just as the merchants of gold and precious gems are meticulous to the utmost precision in weighing them due to their precious value. For the fruits of the commandments are the true perfection and the eternal preciousness of which there is nothing more precious.

To summarize what we have learned, the primary [purpose] of man's existence in this world is solely to fulfill the commandments, serve [G-d] and stand up to trials.

The pleasures of this world should only be used for aiding and assisting him, so that he will have tranquility and peace of mind in order to free his heart for this service incumbent upon him.

Thus it is proper that all of a man's inclination be solely to the blessed Creator and that all of his actions great or small have no other purpose than to draw closer to G-d, blessed be He, and to break down all the barriers separating him from his Master, which are all the matters of physicality and the things dependent on them, until he is drawn towards the blessed G-d like iron is drawn to a magnet.

And anything that he deems to be a means serving to drawing close to G-d, he will chase after it, grab hold of it, and not let it go.

And anything which he deems to be detrimental to this, he should flee from it as one flees from fire, similar to what is written: "my soul clings after You. Your right hand upholds me" (Ps. 63:9).

For his coming to this world is only for this purpose, namely, to attain this closeness, by rescuing his soul from whatever hindrance and detriment to it.

Behold, after we have known this general principle and clarified its veracity, we must investigate on its details, according to its stages, from beginning to end as Rabbi Pinchas ben Yair arranged in his teaching which we brought in the introduction. These steps are "watchfulness", "zeal", "cleanliness", "separation", "purity", "piety", "humility", "fear of sin", "holiness".

Now we will clarify them one by one, with G-d's help.

Messulat   Chapter 1   **Yesharim**

Messilat Yesharim

Chapter 2

The idea of watchfulness is for one to be cautious of his deeds and matters, namely, contemplating and watching over his deeds and ways whether they are good or evil; not abandoning his soul to the danger of destruction, G-d forbid, and not walking through the course of habit like a blind man in darkness.

Reason certainly obligates this. For after a person has knowledge and reason to save himself and escape from the destruction of his soul, how is it conceivable that he would willingly blind his eyes from saving himself?!

There is certainly no debasement and foolishness worse than this. One who does this is lower than beasts and wild animals whose nature it is to protect themselves, escaping and fleeing from whatever seems harmful to them.

One who walks along in his world without contemplating whether his ways are good or evil is similar to a blind man walking on the bank of a river. His danger is certainly very great and his calamity is more likely than his escape. For negligence in guarding oneself from danger due to natural blindness and negligence due to willful blindness, namely shutting one's eyes by choice and desire is one and the same.

Jeremiah would bemoan on the evil of his contemporaries' affliction with the disease of this trait. They would turn a blind eye to their deeds, not putting heart to consider what they were doing, whether to do or refrain from doing it.

Regarding them he said: "no man regrets of his evil, saying. What have I done? Each one running to his own course, as the horse rushes into the battle." (Jer. 8:6)

The explanation is that they would pursue and go by the momentum of habit and conduct, without leaving themselves time to consider their deeds and ways. Thus they fell into evil without even seeing it.

In truth, this is one of the cunning strategies of the evil inclination, to relentlessly burden people's hearts with his service so as to leave them no room to reflect and consider which road they are taking.

For he knows that if they were to put their ways to heart even the slightest bit, certainly they would immediately begin to feel regret for their deeds. The remorse would go and intensify within them until they would abandon the sin completely.

This is similar to the wicked Pharaoh's advice saying "intensify the men's labor..." (Ex. 5:9). His intention was to leave them no time whatsoever to oppose him or plot against him. He strove to confound their hearts of all reflection by means of the constant, incessant labor.

This is precisely the ploy employed by the evil inclination on human beings. For he is a skilled warrior, expert in the art of cunning. It is impossible to escape from him without great wisdom and far-reaching vision. This is what the prophet screamed out "give heed to your ways!" (Chagai 1:7).

And as Shlomo in his wisdom said: "Give not sleep to your eyes, nor slumber to your eyelids. Save yourself as a deer from the hand of the hunter and as a bird from the hand of the fowler" (Prov. 6:4).

And our sages of blessed memory said "whoever scrutinizes his ways in this world merits to see the salvation of the holy One blessed be He".

And it is obvious that even if one is watchful over himself, it is not within his power to save himself without the help of the holy One blessed be He. For the evil inclination is enormously powerful as scripture says: "the wicked watches the righteous, and seeks to slay him, G-d will not forsake him to his power" (Ps. 37:32).

If a man is watchful over himself, then the holy One blessed be He helps him and he will be saved from the evil inclination.

But if he is not watchful over himself, the Holy One, blessed be He, will certainly not watch over him. For if he gives no heed to himself, who should give heed to him? This is as our Sages of blessed memory have said: "it is forbidden to pity anyone who has no knowledge" (Berachot 33a), and this is the meaning of what they said: "if I am not for myself, who will be for me?" (Avot 1:14).

Messilat Yesharim

Chapter 3

He who wants to watch over himself must investigate two matters.

The first: that he contemplates what is the true good for man to choose and what is the true evil for him to flee from.

The second: on the actions which he does, to determine if they are in the category of the good or the evil.

This applies both to times when he is in the act of doing and when not in the act of doing.

When in the act of doing: that he not do any act without first weighing it on the scales of this understanding.

Not in the act of doing: that he bring up before himself the remembrance of his deeds in general and weigh them, likewise, in these scales to determine what they contain of evil in order to relinquish it and what of good, in order to perpetuate it and strengthen himself in it. If he finds in them of the evil, he should then contemplate and investigate, reasoning out a strategy to employ in order to turn away from that evil and cleanse himself of it.

Our sages, of blessed memory, taught us this in their saying: "it would have been preferable for a person had he not been created, but now that he has been created let him examine (pishpush) his deeds; others say: let him feel out (mashmesh) his deeds" (Eruvin 13a). See how these two terms are two very good and beneficial instructions.

"Examining" (pishpush) of deeds is to investigate generally one's deeds and inspect them to see whether they contain deeds which one does not do, namely, that are not in line with the commandments of G-d and His statutes. All that he finds of these, he should eradicate them from the world.

"Feeling out" (mishmush) of deeds, on the other hand, is investigation even on the good deeds themselves to inspect and see if they contain any leaning which is not good or any evil component which he needs to remove and eradicate.

This is analogous to feeling out a garment to ascertain whether it is good and strong or weak and frayed. So too, he should feel out his deeds to ascertain their nature through an absolutely thorough examination until they are left pure and clean.

The general principle: that a man inspects all of his deeds and watch over all of his ways to not leave for himself any bad habit or bad trait, all the more so any transgression or sin.

I see a need for a man to be meticulous and weigh his ways each and every day like the great merchants who continuously evaluate all of their business matters in order that they not degenerate. He should fix definite times and hours for this weighing so that it not be haphazard but rather with the greatest regularity for it yields great results.

Our sages of blessed memory taught us explicitly the need for this accounting as they said (Bava Batra 78b):

"'therefore, the rulers said, let us enter into an accounting' (Numbers 21:27). Therefore, the rulers - of their [evil] inclinations said come and consider the accounting of the world - the loss incurred by doing a mitzva against the gain earned through it, and the gain obtained by doing a sin against the loss incurred..."

This true counsel could not have been given nor could its truth be recognized except by those who had already gone out of the hands of their evil inclination and ruled over it. For one who is still held captive in the prison of his evil inclination - his eyes do not see this truth, and he is incapable of recognizing it. For the evil inclination literally blinds his eyes. He is like one walking in darkness, where there are stumbling blocks before him but his eyes do not see them.

This is what our sages said: "'You make darkness, and it is night' (Ps. 104:20) - this refers to this world which is analogous to night." (Bava Metzia 83b).

How wondrous is this truthful statement to one who delves deeply to understand it. For behold the darkness of night causes man's eyes to err in two ways. (1) it covers the eye so that he cannot see at all what is before him. (2) Or it deceives him so that a pillar appears as if it is a man or a man as a pillar.

So too, the material and physicality of this world - behold it is darkness of night to the eye of the intellect, and causes him to err on two fronts:

First, it prevents him from seeing the stumbling blocks standing in the ways of this world.

Thus, the simpletons walk confidently, fall and are lost without having felt any prior fear. This is what scripture refers to: "the way of the wicked is as darkness; they know not at what they stumble" (Prov. 4:19), and "the clever one foresees the evil and hides himself, but the foolish commits transgression and is punished" (Prov. 22:3), and "[a wise one fears and departs from evil], but the fool transgresses and feels confident" (Prov 14:16). For they feel as secure as an edifice, and they fall before having any knowledge whatsoever of the stumbling block.

The second error, and this is even worse than the first, is that [the darkness] distorts their sight until they literally see evil as if it were good and good as if it were evil. Thus they strengthen in clenching to their evil ways. For not only do they lack the [proper] vision to see the truth, to perceive the evil right in front of their eyes, but they also see fit to conjure up great proofs and convincing evidences to support their evil logic and false ideas.

This is the great evil which envelopes them and clings to them, carrying them to the abyss of destruction. This is what scripture states: "the heart of this people has become fattened, and its ears heavy, their eyes covered shut; lest they see with their eyes, and hear with their ears, and understand with their hearts, and turn back, and be healed" (Isaiah 6:10).

All this is due to their being under [the influence of] darkness and held captive under the dominion of their evil inclination. But those who already escaped from this prison are able to see the truth clearly and can counsel other people on it.

To what is this analogous? To a labyrinth. This is a garden planted for amusement, commonly known to the noblemen. The hedges of plants are arranged into many intricate walls, among them many confusing and interlacing pathways, all of which appear similar.

The goal is to reach the lookout tower in the midst of the maze. But among these pathways some of them truly lead one to the tower while others deceive him, leading him to stray away from it.

One who walks between the paths is not at all capable of seeing or knowing if he is walking along a correct path or a deceptive one. For each one appears similar, there is no noticeable difference whatsoever to the eye beholding them. He will not reach the tower unless he knows the correct path through prior experience and visual familiarity by having entered it before and successfully reached the goal, namely, the tower.

One standing on the lookout tower, on the other hand, can see all of the pathways before him and discern between the true and false ones. He is in a position to warn those walking in them and tell them: "this is the path to take!".

He that is willing to believe him will reach the designated place. But he who is not willing to believe him, but would rather follow his own eyes, will certainly remain lost and fail to reach it.

So too here, one who still has not ruled over his evil inclination is lost in the midst of the "pathways" and cannot distinguish between them. But those who rule over their evil inclination, who have already reached the tower and left the pathways and who clearly see all the pathways before their eyes - they can counsel those who are willing to listen. It is these people that we must trust.

And what is the counsel they give us? "Let us enter into an accounting, come and consider the accounting of the world". For they already experienced, saw and learned, that this alone is the true path leading a man to the good which he seeks, and that there is none other besides this.

The summary of all the matter is that a man must contemplate with his intellect always, at all times, and also during the fixed appointed time of solitude, what is the true path according to the Torah that man must walk upon. And afterwards, to come to reflect on his own deeds to ascertain if they are traveling in this path or not. For through this certainly it will be easy for him to purify himself of all evil, and to correct all of his ways as scripture says: "Weigh the path of your feet, and all your ways will be established" (Prov. 4:26) and "Let us search and examine our ways, and we will return to G-d" (Eicha 3:40).

Messulat Chapter 3 Yesharim

Messilat Yesharim

Chapter 4

Generally, that which brings a person to watchfulness is the study of Torah as Rabbi Pinchas ben Yair stated in the Beraitha: "Torah brings to Watchfulness."

But that which, in particular, brings one to watchfulness is contemplation on the severity of the service which a man is obligated in and the depth of judgment incurred for it. This realization comes from studying the events reported in the holy books, and from studying the statements of our Sages of blessed memory which rouse one on this.

This reflection has varying degrees of arousing, respectively, for those of wholeness of understanding, those of lesser understanding, and for the general masses. Those of wholeness of understanding will be roused to watchfulness by their coming to see clearly that only perfection and nothing else is worthy of their desire, and that there is no greater evil than the lack of perfection and distance from it.

For after this has become clear to them and likewise after it has become clear to them that the means to perfection are good deeds and traits, they will certainly never consent to diminish these means or be lenient in them. Since, it has already become clear to them that if they diminish in these means or are weak in these means, not employing the full force necessary, they will not attain the true perfection. Rather, it will be reduced in proportion to their reduction in exerting themselves to the necessary extent, leaving them lacking in perfection which is a great calamity and great evil to them.

Therefore, they will choose only to maximize these means and to be stringent in all of their details, finding no rest or peace due to worry lest they possibly lack what will bring them to the perfection that they desire. This is what King Shlomo, peace be unto him, said: "fortunate is the man that fears always" (Mishlei 28:14), which our Sages explained (Berachot 60a) refers to matters of Torah.

The pinnacle of this level called "fear of sin", one of the greatest levels, is when a man is constantly afraid and worried lest he have in his hand some trace of sin which obstructs him from the perfection that he is under duty to strive for.

Regarding this our Sages of blessed memory said: "this teaches each person is burned from the Chupa (canopy) of his fellow" (Bava Basra 75a). This [burning] does not refer to jealousy which falls only to people lacking in understanding as I will explain with G-d's help. Rather, it is due to seeing oneself lacking from the perfection that he was capable of attaining just as his fellow had attained it.

Through this contemplation certainly one of wholeness of understanding will not refrain from being watchful of his deeds.

Those of lesser understanding, however, will be roused to Watchfulness according to their perceptions. Namely, according to the matter of honor that they crave.

For it is evident to every man of faith, that the various levels in the world of truth, i.e., the world to come, are according to one's level of deeds and that one is only elevated over his fellow if his deeds are greater than his fellow's, but one who is of few deeds will be the lower one.

If so, how could a man hide his eye from his deeds or slacken his striving in attaining this? For afterwards, certainly he will suffer at the time he can no longer rectify what he made crooked.

There are some simpletons who seek only to lighten the burden on themselves. They reply: "why should we weary ourselves with so much Piety and Separation? Is it not sufficient for us to not be among the wicked sentenced to Gehinom? We will not strain ourselves just to enter into the innermost chambers of Gan Eden. If we don't have a large portion, at least we will have a small portion.

This is enough for us. We will not further burden the yoke of our load just for this."

There is just one question that we will put to these people: can they so easily tolerate in this fleeting world the sight of one their peers being honored and elevated above them, and coming to rule over them? Or worse still, if this is one of their servants or one of the beggars which are lowly and despicable in their eyes. Would they not be filled with pain and would their blood not boil inside them?. Surely, they could not!

For behold we can see with our own eyes that all of a man's labor is to raise himself over anyone he can and to establish his place among those more elevated. This is jealousy between man and his fellow. For if he sees his fellow being elevated while he remains lowly, certainly what he tolerates will be only what he is forced to tolerate because of his inability to prevent it, but his heart will rot within him.

Hence if it is so difficult for them to be lower than their fellow in levels that are imaginary and false, where a lower level is just a superficial appearance, and all elevation is just vanity and falsehood. How then will they tolerate seeing themselves lower than those same people who are now their inferiors? And this is in the place of true levels and eternal worth, which even though they don't recognize it and its worth now, therefore they don't give much concern for it, but in its time, certainly, they will understand it for what it truly is, to their pain and shame. There is no doubt, that their suffering in this will be enormous and everlasting.

Hence, this "tolerance" which they adopt in order to lighten on themselves the severity of the service is but a deceit which their evil inclination employs to incite them, with no basis whatsoever in truth.

There would be no room for this incitement if they saw the truth of the matter, but since they do not seek the truth, but go on in their erroneous ways willingly, this incitement will not leave them until the time when it will no longer avail. For it will not be in their power to rectify what they had ruined. This is what King Shlomo, peace be unto him, referred to: "Whatever your hand finds to do with your power, do it, for there is no deed, nor account, nor knowledge, nor wisdom [in the She'ol (grave) where you are going]" (Ecc.9:10).

The explanation is that: what a man can do while the power is granted in his hands by the Creator, namely, the power of free will granted to him all the days of his life with which he chooses and is commanded to do, behold he will not be able to do more in the grave and pit. For this power [of free will] will no longer be in his hands. Thus one who has failed to do many good deeds in his lifetime, it is impossible for him to do them afterwards (since he no longer has free will after death). And he who did not make an accounting of his deeds [while alive] will no longer have the opportunity to do it then. And he who has not become wise in this world, will not become wise in the grave. This is the intent of: "for there is no deed nor account nor knowledge in the She'ol were you are going" (Ecc.9:10).

But the general masses will be roused to "Watchfulness" through the matter of reward and punishment upon recognizing the extent of the depth of judgment on this. In truth, it is proper to continuously shudder and fear, for who will stand on the Day of Judgment? Who will be found righteous before his Creator, whose sight scrutinizes all things, great and small.

Likewise, our Sages of blessed memory said on the verse: "Who declares to man his speech" (Amos 4:13) - "even casual talk between a man and his wife is related to a man at the time of judgment" (Chagiga 5b).

And expounding on "it is very stormy round about Him" (Ps. 50:3) - "this teaches that the Holy One blessed be He scrutinizes judgment on His pious ones to the degree of a hair's breadth" (Yevamos 121a).

Avraham, who was so beloved to his Maker such that scripture testifies of him "Avraham, My beloved" (Isaiah 41:8). Even so, he did not escape from judgment for slight words which he was not meticulous in, namely, for merely saying "with what will I know?" (Gen. 15:8), G-d replied to him: "by your life, you will know that your descendants will be foreigners [in Egypt]" (Nedarim 32a). And similarly, for forging a covenant with Abimelech without being commanded by G-d, the Holy One blessed be He, replied to him: "by your life, I will delay the rejoicing of your sons for seven generations" (Gen. Raba 54:5).

Yaakov, for replying angrily to Rachel when she said to him "give me children", the Midrash reports (Genesis Raba 71:10): "the Holy One blessed be He, said to him: 'is this how one answers a distressed person? By your life, your sons will stand before her son'.

And for hiding his daughter Dina in a box so that his brother Esav would not take her as a wife, even though his intent was certainly good, but nevertheless for merely withholding kindness from his brother the Midrash reports: "the Holy One blessed be He said to him: 'He who withholds kindness from his fellow.' (Job 6:14). You did not seek to marry her to a circumcised? Behold she will be married to an uncircumcised. You did not seek to marry her in a permitted way? She will be married in a forbidden way".

Yosef, for saying to the officer of [Pharaoh's] drink: "But remember me when it is well with you [and please show kindness to me, and make mention of me to Pharaoh.]" (Gen 40:14), his sentence [in prison] was increased by 2 years as the Midrash reports (Genesis Raba 89b). And Yosef himself for embalming his father without G-d's permission, according to one view, or because he heard the words: "your servant, our father [Yaakov]" (Gen.43:28) and remained silent, according to another view, died before all of his brothers (Gen. Raba 100:4).

David, because he referred to the words of Torah as "songs", was punished by the calamity of Uza and his joy was muted (Sotah 35a).

Michal, for rebuking David for dancing outside before the Ark was punished by not having children during her lifetime and dying in childbirth (Shmuel II 6:20).

Hizkiyahu, because he showed the treasure house to the ministers of the king of Babylonia, it was decreed that his sons be castrated servants (eunuchs) in the palace of the King of Babylonia (Kings II 20:13).

There are many more instances like this.

In the chapter "All are Liable" (Chagiga 5a): "When Rabbi Yochanan would come to this verse, he would weep - 'I will come near you to judgment and I will be a swift witness...' (Malachi 3:5) - a servant whose minor offenses are weighed just like major offenses, is there any remedy for him?

Certainly the intent is not that the punishment is identical for both, for the Holy One blessed be He only pays back measure for measure. Rather, regarding the matter of weighing of deeds, the minor deeds are put on the scales just like the grave ones. For the grave ones do not cause the minor ones to be forgotten, and the Judge will not overlook these at all just like he will not overlook the grave ones.

Rather on all of them, he will preside over and inspect equally, judging each one and meting out punishment afterwards on each and every one according to what it is. This is what Shlomo said: "For G-d will bring every deed into judgment, [with every hidden thing, whether it be good, or whether it be evil]" (Kohelet 12:14). For just like the Holy One blessed be He does not leave any good deed unrewarded, small as it may be, so too He does not leave any bad deed unjudged and unpunished, small as it may be.

This is to awaken the hearts of those who want to be seduced [by their evil inclination] into thinking that the L-rd, blessed be He, will not bring up in his judgments the minute deeds and will not exact an accounting for them. Rather the general principle is "whoever says the Holy One blessed be He overlooks things will have his life overlooked" (Bava Kama 50a). Likewise, they said: "if the evil inclination says to you: 'sin and the Holy One, blessed be He, will forgive you' - do not listen to him" (Chagiga 16a).

All this is evident and clear for G-d is a G-d of truth as Moshe Rabeinu, peace be unto him, said: "The Rock, His work is perfect; For all His ways are justice: A G-d of faithfulness and without iniquity, Just and right is He" (Deut. 32:4). For since the Holy One blessed be He desires justice, to ignore the bad would be just as much an injustice as to ignore the good. Therefore, if it is justice that He desires, then He must pay each man according to his ways and according to the fruits of his deeds to absolute exactness, whether for good or for bad. Thus "A G-d of faithfulness and without iniquity, Just and right is He" (Deut. 32:4) which our Sages of blessed memory explained [the dual terms]: "to the righteous and to the wicked" (Taanis 11a). For this is the trait [of justice]. He judges on every thing. He punishes every sin. And there is no escape.

If you ask: if so, for what does G-d's attribute of mercy exist if He must be absolutely meticulous in judging every thing? The answer: The trait of mercy is certainly the pillar of the world. For it could not endure without it at all whatsoever. But nevertheless, G-d's attribute of justice is not negated. For according to strict justice it would be proper that:

- the sinner be punished immediately for his sin without any delay whatsoever.

- that the punishment itself be wrathful as befits one who rebels against the word of the Creator, blessed be His Name.

- that there be no possible repair whatsoever for the sin.

For in truth, how can a man rectify what he has made crooked after committing the sin? If one murdered his fellow or committed adultery? How can he possibly rectify this? Can he undo a deed already done from existence?

But the attribute of mercy reverses the three aforementioned matters.

- it grants that the sinner be given time and not be eradicated from the earth immediately upon sinning.

- that the punishment itself not utterly destroy him.

- that the opportunity of repentance be granted to sinners as a complete kindness, so that the uprooting of the will be counted as the uprooting of the deed.

Thus when the penitent man recognizes his sin and admits it, and reflects on his evil, repents of it and completely regrets ever having done it, as he would regret [in annulling] a certain vow, in which case there is complete regret, and he desires and longs that this deed had never been committed, and pains himself strongly that the matter was done, and renounces it for the future, and flees from it - then the uprooting of the deed from his will is counted to him as the annulment of a vow and he gains atonement for it. As scripture says: "your iniquity is gone and your sin atoned for" (Isaiah 6:7) - that the sin is actually removed from existence, and uprooted through his paining himself and regretting in the present what he had done in the past.

This is certainly a kindness for it is not according to the letter of justice. But nevertheless, it does not negate the attribute of justice completely for there are ways to consider it justice.

- For in place of the will to consent to sin, and the pleasure that it provided, there is now regret and pain.

- Providing him time is not an overlooking of the sin, but rather a small patience, to open for him an opening to rectify.

- So too, for all the ways of kindliness, such as "a son brings merit to the father" (Sanhedrin 104a), or "part of a life like the whole of a life" (Kohelet Raba 7:25) mentioned by the Sages which are aspects of kindness to account a small amount as a large amount. But these do not really conflict with or contradict the attribute of justice. For there is already a proper reason to consider them [as justice].

But to let sins pass without any reason or to ignore them - this would be completely against justice. For this would not constitute a truthful justice in the matter. Therefore, it is impossible for this to be found at all. Hence, if one of the ways mentioned above is not found for the sinner to escape, certainly, the attribute of justice will not return empty. Likewise, our Sages of blessed memory said: "He withholds wrath but collects what is His" (Bereishis Raba 67:4).

We find therefore, that a man who wants to open his eyes does not have any valid enticement to prevent him from being watchful of his deeds to the utmost watchfulness, and to examine them to the utmost scrutiny. Indeed, all these investigations which if one considers will certainly acquire through them the trait of watchfulness if he is a conscientious person (baal nefesh).

Messulat Chapter 4 Yesharim

Messilat Yesharim

Chapter 5

There are three factors which cause loss of and distancing from "watchfulness".

The first is involvement and preoccupation in worldly affairs. The second is laughter and levity. The third is bad company. We will discuss each one in turn.

Regarding worldly involvement and preoccupation, we have already spoken about this earlier. For while a man is occupied in his worldly affairs, his thoughts are bound by the chains of the burden that weighs on them and it is impossible for him to give thought to his deeds.

Considering this, our sages, peace be unto them, said: "minimize your worldly occupations and toil in the Torah" (Avot 4:12).

Occupying oneself to obtain a livelihood is indeed necessary but it is not necessary to occupy oneself to such an extent that he has no room left for service [of G-d]. For this we were commanded to fix times for Torah study.

We have already pointed out that this is the most essential of all things for the acquiring of watchfulness, as the

Beraitha of Rabbi Pinchas ben Yair states: "Torah brings to watchfulness". Without Torah, one will not reach it at all. This is what our sages said "an ignorant man cannot be pious" (Avot 2:6).

For the Creator, blessed be He, who created the evil inclination also created the Torah as its antidote as our sages of blessed memory have stated: "I have created the evil inclination, and I have created the Torah as its antidote" (Kidushin 30b).

Behold, it is obvious that if the Creator created for this affliction only this remedy, then it is impossible under any circumstances for a man to heal himself from this affliction without employing this treatment. One who thinks to save himself without Torah study is only mistaken, and will see his error only in the end, when he dies in sin.

For in truth, the evil inclination is exceedingly powerful on a man. Without a man's knowledge, it advances and strengthens over him and comes to rule over him. Even if he employs all possible strategies in the world, but does not take the medication created for it, namely, the Torah as I wrote, he will not know nor feel the intensification of his illness until he dies in sin and his soul will be lost.

To what can this be likened? To the case of a sick person who consulted the doctors. They recognized his illness, and prescribed for him the healing medication. But he, without any prior knowledge of medicine, disregards their medication and instead takes whatever medicine that occurs to him. Will not this sick person certainly die?

So too in our case, for no one recognizes the illness of the evil inclination and its powers except for the Creator who created it. And He Himself cautioned us that the only remedy for it is Torah. Who then will abandon it, take something else instead and expect to live. Certainly, the darkness of the physical will advance and strengthen over him level after level, without his realizing it until he finds himself immersed in evil, so distantly far from the truth that even thoughts of seeking [the truth] will not enter his heart.

But if he toils in the Torah, when he sees its ways, commandments, and warnings, behold, on its own, eventually a renewal will awaken within him which will bring him to the good path. This is what our sages of blessed memory stated: "would that it were that they abandoned Me but kept My Torah, for the light within it would bring them back to the good" (Eicha Raba 2).

Included in this, is also to fix daily times for the accounting of deeds and their correction as I mentioned earlier.

Besides all this, all the free time he has left from his affairs, if he is wise, certainly he should not waste it. But rather to immediately grasp hold of it and not be lax in it, utilizing it to toil in the affairs of his soul and the improvement of his service of G-d.

Although this detrimental factor we have discussed is the most prevalent, nevertheless it is the easiest to escape from, for he who wants to escape it.

The second detrimental factor, laughter and levity, is very severe. For one who is immersed in these is like one immersed in the great sea, from which it is extremely difficult to escape. For behold, laughter destroys a man's heart until reason and knowledge no longer rule in him. He becomes like a drunkard or a madman whereby it is impossible to give counsel or guide them for they are incapable of accepting any direction.

This was said by King Shlomo, peace be unto him: "I said of laughter, it is madness; and of merriment, what use is it?" (Ecc. 2:2). And the Sages of blessed of memory, said: "laughter and light-headedness habituate a person to illicit relations" (Avot 3:13). For even though sexual immorality is regarded as severe by every man of faith, and his heart fears approaching it, due to the vivid picture that has been imprinted in his mind of the enormity of the sin and the severe punishment it incurs, nevertheless, laughter and light-headedness draw him on little by little, advancing him nearer till the fear of sin leaves him bit by bit, degree after degree, until he reaches the sin itself and commits it.

Why is this so? Because just like the essence of "watchfulness" involves putting matters to mind, so the essence of laughter is to remove from one's mind straight, rational thinking so that thoughts of fearing G-d do not enter his heart at all.

Consider the severity of levity and its destructive power. For just like a shield smeared with oil deflects and drops arrows from him, causing them to fall to the ground, preventing them from reaching the body of the man, so too is levity before rebuke and reprimand. For with one act of levity or a little laughter, a man casts from himself a great many rousings and impressions that the heart was made to feel due to stimulation in seeing or hearing matters that awakened him to an accounting and examination of his deeds.

The power of levity knocks it all to the ground thus not making any impression whatsoever on him. This is not due to the ineffectiveness of the matters nor to lack of understanding on his part, but rather to the power of levity which demolishes all matters of Mussar (ethics) and fear of G-d.

Behold, the prophet Isaiah would "scream like a crane" for he saw that this was what left no room for his rebukes to make an impression thus ruining all hope for the sinners. This is what he said: "And now do not be mockers lest your afflictions be strengthened" (Isaiah 28:22).

And our sages of blessed memory have already proclaimed: "one who is given to levity brings afflictions on himself" (Avodah Zara 18b). And scripture states explicitly: "Judgments are prepared for the frivolous" (Prov. 19:29). This is something reason dictates. For one who is aroused through reflection and study does not need the ordeal of bodily sufferings since he will repent of his sins even without this. He repents by means of thoughts of repentance awakening in his heart stimulated by the reading or hearing the reprimands and rebukes.

But the frivolous are not impacted by the rebukes due to the power of levity. Therefore, there is no way to rectify them except through sufferings. For they are not capable of deflecting the impact of sufferings through the power of levity like they do so with the rebukes.

According to the severity of the sin and its consequences, the True Judge increased its punishment as our sages of blessed memory taught us: "levity is extremely severe; it starts with suffering and ends in utter destruction as written (Isaiah 28:22):'And now do not be mockers lest your bonds be strengthened for a decree of destruction have I heard...' " (Avodah Zara 18b).

The third detrimental factor is [evil] company, namely, the company of fools and sinners. This is what scriptures says: "he who befriends the fools will be broken" (Prov.13:20). We can see many times, even after the truth of a man's duty for divine service and watchfulness of it has been established by him, he becomes lax in it or transgresses certain commandments so that his friends do not mock him or in order to be able to mingle freely in their company.

This is the intent of Shlomo's warning: "do not mingle with those who make changes" (Prov.24:21). If a man claims to you: "a person's mind should always be associated with his fellow men" (Ketuvot 17a), reply to him, "this refers to human beings who act like human beings. Not human beings who act like animals." Shlomo warns further: "Go from before a foolish man" (Prov. 14:7). And King David said: "Fortunate is the man that walks not in the counsel of the wicked, nor stands in the way of sinners, nor sits in the seat of scoffers" (Ps. 1:1). Our sages expounded this: "If he walks, he will eventually stand. If he stood, he will eventually sit" (Avodah Zara 18b). And "I did not sit with men of falsehood, neither did I go with hypocrites. I have hated the congregation of evil-doers, and will not sit with the wicked" (Ps. 26:4-5).

A man has no [remedy] but to purify and cleanse himself and to refrain his feet from the ways of the masses who are sunken in the vanities of the time and to redirect his feet to the courtyards of G-d and His sanctuaries. This is what David himself concludes: "I will wash my hands in cleanliness and I will go around Your altar, O G-d" (Ps. 26:6).

If he happens to find himself in the company of those who mock him, he should not give heart to this mockery. On the contrary, let him mock them and shame them. Let him consider in his heart - if he had an opportunity to profit a great amount of money, would he leave what he needed to do for this due to other people's mocking him? How much more so, to not want to lose his soul for the sake of sparing himself some mockery.

In this manner the sages of blessed memory warned us: "be brazen as a leopard... to do the will of your Father in Heaven" (Avot 5:20). And David said: "I will speak of Your testimonies before kings, and will not be ashamed" (Ps. 119:46).

Even though most kings' occupation and speech is in matters of grand accomplishments and pleasures and David who was also a king, would seem to be embarrassed to speak words of Torah and ethics while in their company instead of great feats and pleasures like them. Nevertheless, he did not care at all. His heart was not enticed for these vanities after he had already attained the truth. Rather, he states explicitly: "I will speak of Your testimonies before kings, and will not be ashamed". Likewise, Isaiah says: "I have set My face like a flint, and I know that I shall not be ashamed" (Isaiah 50:7).

Messilat Yesharim

Chapter 6

After "watchfulness" comes "zeal". For "watchfulness" revolves around the negative mitzvot while "zeal" around the positive mitzvot. This is as written "turn from evil and do good" (Ps. 34:15).

The matter of "Zeal" is clear. It is the early engaging in mitzvot and their completion as the sages of blessed memory said: "the zealous are early to perform the mitzvot" (Pesachim 4a).

For just like it requires great intelligence and much foresight to save oneself from the snares of the evil inclination, and to escape from the evil so that it does not rule over us and mix in our deeds, so too it requires great cleverness and foresight to grasp the mitzvot, to acquire them, and not to lose them.

For just like the evil inclination causes and strives with its strategies to cast man into the nets of sin, so too it strives to prevent him from performing Mitzvot and to leave him devoid of them.

If a man weakens and is lazy, not strengthening himself to pursue them and to hold on to them, he will certainly remain shaken out and empty of them.

You can observe that man's nature weighs very heavily upon him. For the earthiness of the physical is gross. Therefore, a man does not want to exert himself and labor. But he who wants to merit to the service of the Creator must strengthen himself against his own nature, mustering strength and zeal.

If he leaves himself in the hands of his [natural] heaviness, it is a certainty that he will not succeed. This is what the Tana (Mishnaic sage) stated: "be brazen as a leopard, light as an eagle, swift as a deer, and mighty as a lion to do the will of your Father in Heaven" (Avot 5:20). Likewise, the Sages counted among the things which need strengthening: "Torah and good deeds" (Berachot 32b). This is explicitly stated in scripture: "be strong and very courageous [to observe and do all of the Torah...]" (Yehoshua 1:6). For great strengthening is needed for one who wants to bend his nature to its opposite.

Behold, Shlomo repeatedly exhorted many times on this in seeing the evil of laziness and the greatness of the harm resulting from it. He said "a little sleep, a little slumber, a little folding of the hands to rest. Then shall your poverty come as a traveler" (Mishlei 24:33). For behold, even though the lazy person is not doing evil actively, nevertheless he brings evil on himself through his very inactivity.

Shlomo further said: "also he who is slack in his work is a brother to the destroyer" (Mishlei 18:9). For even though this person is not a destroyer who commits evil directly with his own hands, don't think he is far removed from being one. On the contrary, he is the destroyer's brother and his comrade.

He further stated a familiar, every day illustration to explain the evil that befalls the lazy person: "I passed by the field of a lazy man, and by the vineyard of the man without understanding; And, lo, it was all grown over with thorns, and nettles had covered the face of it, and its stone wall was broken down; Then I observed; I put my heart to it; I beheld and I received mussar (instruction); A little sleep, a little slumber, a little folding of the hands to lie down; so shall your poverty come as a traveler, and your want like a man with a shield" (Mishlei 24:30-34).

Besides the plain meaning, which is true in the literal sense, for this is indeed what happens to the field of a lazy man, the sages of blessed memory expounded it beautifully in a Midrash (Yalkut Mishlei 247:961) as follows:

"it was all grown over with thorns" - refers to one who seeks the interpretation of a portion of the Torah and does not find it.

"nettles had covered the face of it" - since he did not labor sufficiently in the Torah, he sits in judgment and declares the pure, unclean and the impure, clean, thus breaching the fence set up by the Torah Sages. What is his punishment? Shlomo revealed it: "one who breaches a fence will be bitten by a snake" (Kohelet 10:8).

That is, the evil that befalls the lazy man does not come all at once. Rather it comes little by little. Without his knowing it or sensing it, he is pulled from one evil to another until he finds himself sunk in ultimate evil.

Behold, at first, he is merely diminishing the labor that was proper for him. This draws him to not study the Torah adequately. Due to lack of study, when he goes afterwards to study, he will be lacking the requisite understanding.

If the evil that befalls him would end there, his calamity would already be great. But it grows further, for in his desire to at least explain the section or chapter under consideration, he distorts reasons not in accordance with Halacha, destroying truth, and perverting it till he transgresses decrees and breaches the fences.

His end is destruction like all those who breach fences. Shlomo continues: "then I observed; I put my heart to it" - I reflected on this matter and realized the great evil in it, for it is like a poison which creeps and spreads little by little. Its effect is not noticed until death comes. This is the meaning of: "a little sleep... so shall your destitution come swiftly as a traveler, etc."

We can observe with our own eyes how so often a person comes to understand his duty in this world and grasps the truth of what is required to save his soul and what is his duty towards his Creator, but despite this, he disregards it. This disregard is not due to insufficient clarity of this duty, nor any other cause but the heaviness of laziness which overcomes him.

He thus says: "I will eat a bit", or "I will sleep a little", or "it is difficult for me to leave my house". "I have put off my coat; how shall I put it on again?". "It is very hot outside". "It is very cold" or "it is raining" and all the other sorts of excuses and rationalizations that the mouths of lazy people are full of. Either way, in the meantime the Torah is abandoned, the service of G-d is idle, and man abandons his Creator. This is what Shlomo said: "by laziness the ceiling decays; and through lowering of the hands the house leaks" (Kohelet 10:18).

If you ask the lazy person [to explain his behavior], he will confront you with numerous quotations of the sages, verses from scripture, and logical arguments all of which instruct him, according to his distorted mind, to be lenient with himself, and to leave himself in the tranquility of his laziness.

But he fails to see that all these arguments and reasons do not stem from balanced reasoning but rather spring from the wellspring of laziness, which, as it strengthens over him, inclines his views and intellect to those arguments. Hence, he fails to heed the voice of the wise and men of sound judgment. This is what Shlomo screams out: "The lazy man is wiser in his own eyes than seven men that answer sensibly" (Mishlei 26:16).

For laziness does not allow him to be even concerned for the words of those who rebuke him. Rather he will consider them all to be mistaken or foolish, while he alone is the wise one.

Know that this is a fundamental principle, well tested by experience, in the art of Separation: every leniency must be carefully investigated. For even though, it is possible that it is justified and correct, nevertheless it is more likely to be the advice of the evil inclination and its deceit. Therefore, one must investigate it with much analysis and examination. If after all this it still stands meritorious, then certainly it is good.

The summary of the matter: a man must greatly strengthen himself and fortify himself with zeal in doing the Mitzvot by casting off himself the weight of laziness which impedes him.

The angels were praised for possessing this good trait as written: "[Bless the L-rd, His angels,] those mighty in strength, who perform His word, hearkening to the voice of His word" (Tehilim 103:20); and "the Chayot dash to and fro like the appearance of a flash of lightning" (Yechezkel 1:14). Behold, a man is a man and not an angel, hence it is impossible for him to attain the might of an angel, but he should certainly strive to do all he can to come as close to that level as possible. King David would praise (G-d) for his portion saying: "I hasten and do not delay to keep your commandments" (Tehilim 119:60).

Messulat　　Chapter 6　　Yesharim

Messilat Yesharim

Chapter 7

There are two divisions of Zeal. One applies before beginning a deed and the other one after beginning a deed.

Before beginning a deed: that one not allows a Mitzva to become delayed (lit. Chametz).

Rather when the time of its performance comes, or when it happens to present itself to him, or when the thought of performing it enters his mind, he should hurry and hasten to seize hold of it and perform it, and not allow time to go by in between. For there is no danger like its danger. Since, behold each new second that arises can bring with it a new impediment to the good deed.

Our sages of blessed memory roused us to the truth of this matter in reference to the coronation of Shlomo. David told Beniyahu (in Melachim 1:33-36) "take him down to Gihon". Beniyahu replied: "Amen, may G-d say so [too]".

The sages taught on this (Midrash Bereishis 76:2): "Rabbi Pinchas in the name of Rabbi Yochanan of Tzipori: was is it not already said: 'Behold, a son shall be born to you who shall be a man of tranquility. [And I will give him peace from all his enemies all around. For his name shall be Shlomo]'(Divrei Hayamim 1-22:9)? [Answer:] Rather, because many prosecutors (mishaps) can arise from here to Gihon.

Therefore, the sages of blessed memory exhorted us: "And you shall watch over the Matzot" - if a Mitzva comes to your hand, do not delay its performance (lit. allow it to become Chametz)' (Mechilta Shemot 12:17).

And they said: "A person should always be quick to do a Mitzvah. For due to Lot's older daughter preceding her sister by one night she merited preceding her by four generations" (Nazir 23b).

And they said: "zealous people do Mitzvot as early as possible" (Pesachim 4a). Likewise, they said: "a person should always run to perform a mitzva, even on the Sabbath".

And in the Midrash (Vayikra Rabba 11:9) on the verse (Tehilim 48:15) "He shall lead us in youth" - [filled] with zeal as young maidens, as it is said: "in the midst of maidens playing the timbrels" (Tehilim 68:26) ["in youth" and "young maidens" are related words in Hebrew].

For the trait of Zeal is a very high spiritual level of Shelemut (perfection) which a person's nature impedes him from attaining at the current time. But he who strengthens himself and takes hold of it as much as he can, will, in the future world, merit to truly attain it. The Creator, may His Name be blessed, will bestow it to him as a reward for his striving for it during the time of his service.

The division of Zeal "after beginning a deed" is as follows. Since one took hold of a mitzva he should hasten to complete it. This is not in order to lighten on himself like one who desires to cast a burden off himself but rather out of fear lest he not merit to complete it.

On this our sages exhorted us numerous times. They said: "one who begins a Mitzva but does not complete it buries his wife and sons" (Bereishis Raba 85:3).

And they said: "a Mitzva is attributed only to the one who completed it" (ibid).

And King Shlomo, peace be unto him, said: "Do you see a man quick in his work? He shall stand before kings; he shall not stand before lowly men" (Mishlei 22:29).

The Sages of blessed memory applied this praise to Shlomo himself for hastening the construction of the Temple and not being lazy in delaying it. They likewise expounded the verse regarding Moshe, peace be unto him, for hastening in the building of the Mishkan (Tabernacle).

Likewise, you will observe that all the deeds of the Tzadikim (righteous) are always performed with haste. By Avraham it is written: "And Abraham hastened into the tent to Sarah, and said, make ready quickly three measures of fine meal... And he gave it to the lad and he hastened to prepare it" (Bereishis 18:6-7)

By Rivka: "and she hastened and emptied her pitcher in the trough..." (Bereishis 24:20).

Likewise, they said in the Midrash (regarding the mother of Shimshon): "'and the woman made haste and ran...' (Shoftim 13:10) (Midrash:) this comes to teach that all the deeds of the righteous are done with haste". For they do not allow an interruption of time to elapse - not before beginning the Mitzva nor in completing it.

You can see that a man whose soul is afire in the service of his Creator certainly will not become lazy in doing the Mitzvot. Rather, his movements will be like the quick movements of fire. For he will not rest nor be still until he has finished completing the deed.

Reflect further that just like an inner fieriness of soul leads one to act with Zeal, so too the opposite, outwardly acting with Zeal leads to an inner fieriness of the soul. Namely, when one feels himself performing a Mitzva with great swiftness this will move his inner being to kindle aflame also, and the desire and want will increasingly intensify within him. But if he acts in a sluggish manner in the movement of his limbs, so too the movement of his spirit will die down and extinguish. This is something experience can testify to.

You already know that what is most desired in the service of G-d, may His Name be blessed, is desire of the heart and longing of the soul. It is concerning this that King David praised his portion saying: "As a deer yearns longingly for the water brooks, so does my soul yearn longingly to You, O G-d; My soul thirsts for G-d..." (Tehilim 42:1-2), "My soul longs, and goes out for the courtyards of G-d" (Tehilim 84:2). "My soul thirsts for You; my flesh longs for You [in an arid and thirsty land (Rashi-desert), without water]"(Tehilim 63:2).

But for a man in whom this longing does not burn as it should, a good advice for him is to act with zeal by force of will in order that this will bring an inner awakening of this longing in his inner nature. For the external movement rouses the inner ones and certainly the external movement is more in his power than the inner ones. Thus, if he exercises what is in his power to do, this will lead him to also attain what is not in his power. For an inner joy will awaken within him and a desire and longing through the power of acting fiery, externally, by the force of will. This is what the prophet said- "let us know, let us run to know the L-rd" (Hoshea 6:3) and "After G-d they will go, who shall roar like a lion"(Hoshea 11:10).

Messilat Yesharim

Chapter 8

The means through which Zeal is acquired are the same ones through which Watchfulness is acquired, and their levels are likewise similar as I wrote earlier.

For their matters are very similar. There is no difference between them except that Zeal is for the positive commandments while Watchfulness is for the negative commandments.

When a man comes to realize as truth the great value of the Mitzvot and the greatness of his obligation in them, his heart will certainly be awakened to the service of G-d and he will not be lax in it.

However, that which may intensify this rousing is looking into the many benefits that the Holy One blessed be He does with a man at all moments and times and the great wonders G-d performs for him from the time of his birth until his final day. For the more one looks into and contemplates these things, the more he will recognize his enormous debt to G-d Who bestows good to him.

This looking into will cause him to not grow lazy or lax in His service. For since it is impossible for him to repay

G-d, blessed be His Name, for His goodness, he will feel that at least he can thank His Name and fulfill His commandments.

Whatever circumstances one may be in, whether poor or rich, healthy or ill, there is no person who cannot see wonders and many great benefits in his particular situation.

For the rich and healthy man is already indebted to G-d, blessed be He, for his wealth and health.

The poor man is indebted to G-d that even in his poverty, G-d provides his sustenance through miracles and wonders, not leaving him to die of hunger.

The sick man [is indebted to G-d] for He strengthens him in the weight of his illness or injuries, and does not leave him to descend to the grave. Likewise, for all similar conditions. There is not a single person who will not find himself indebted to his Creator.

When he looks at these benefits which he receives from G-d, certainly, he will be roused to be Zealous in His service as I wrote earlier.

All the more so, if he contemplates that all of his good is dependent on G-d's hand and that all of his needs and necessities is only from G-d alone, blessed be His Name, and no one else.

Then certainly he will not become lazy from engaging in His Divine service, so that G-d does not diminish that which is essential to him.

Behold, you can see that I included in my words the three levels of people which I divided in relation to Watchfulness for their matters are the same and can be learned one from the other.

Those of wholeness of understanding will be roused to Zeal by their sense of duty and by the great worth and importance of the deeds.

Those of lesser understanding - from matters of the World to Come and honor, so that they do not suffer shame in the Day of Reward in seeing the good he could have attained but lost it.

For the general masses - from matters of this world and its needs similar to what I explained there.

Messilat Yesharim

Chapter 9

The factors which diminish Zeal are those which increase laziness. The greatest of them all is seeking tranquility of body, hatred of exertion and love of [bodily] enjoyments to their fullest extent.

For behold, to a man like this, the service of G-d will certainly weigh very heavily upon him. For one who wishes to eat his meals with full peace and tranquility, to sleep without any disturbance, to walk only at his own leisurely pace, or other similar things, undoubtedly it will be very difficult for him to rise early for synagogue or to cut his meal short so as to pray the afternoon service or to go out to perform a Mitzva if the time is not convenient for him. How much more so, to hurry himself to perform a Mitzva or to study Torah.

One who habituates himself in these practices is not master over himself to do the opposite of these things when he wishes. For his will is already imprisoned in the prison of habit which has become second nature to him.

A man needs to realize that he was not placed in this world for tranquility but rather for toil and exertion. He must conduct himself only as the laborers who perform work for their employers similar to what was said "we are day laborers" (Eruvin 65a) and in the manner of soldiers in their war formations who eat swiftly and sleep irregularly, always ready to engage in battle.

On this scripture says "man was born to toil" (Iyov 5:7). When a man habituates himself in this manner, he will certainly find the service of G-d easy since he does not lack the preparation and readiness for it. Along these lines our sages of blessed memory said "this is the way of Torah, eat bread with salt, drink water in small measure, and sleep on the ground" (Avot 6:4) which is a general statement of distancing to the utmost extreme from the comforts and pleasures.

Another factor which diminishes Zeal is great fear and apprehension of what the future may bring so that sometimes one may fear the cold or the heat. Other times mishaps or illnesses. Other times from the wind and so on and so forth. This is what Shlomo, peace be unto him, said: "The lazy one says there is a lion in the way; a lion is among the streets." (Mishlei 26:13).

The sages already denigrated this trait and attributed it to the sinners, with many verses to support them such as "the sinners in Zion are afraid; trembling has seized the flatterers." (Isaiah 33:14). One of the great sages upon noticing his disciple afraid said to him: "you are a sinner" (Berachot 60a).

On this scripture says: "trust in G-d and do good dwell in the land and be nourished by faith" (Tehilim 37:3).

The summary of the matter is that a man must make himself incidental in worldly matters but fixed in the service of G-d, be content and satisfied in all worldly matters with whatever comes to him, taking what comes to hand, be far from rest and close to toil and exertion, his heart trusting securely in G-d, and not fearing the future and whatever mishaps it may bring.

Perhaps you will say: behold we see that the sages everywhere obligated a man to guard himself well and not put himself in danger even if he is a righteous person with many merits. For instance: "everything is in the hands of heaven except colds and heatstrokes" (Ketubot 30a) and the Torah says "you shall guard yourselves very carefully" (Devarim 4:15). Hence one should not decide to "trust in G-d" in all situations, and in the Talmud Yerushalmi (Berachot 3, see also Chulin 142a) they said: "even when performing a Mitzva!".

Know that there is fear and there is fear. There is justified fear and there is foolish fear. There is trust [in G-d] and there is recklessness.

The L-rd, blessed be He, has made man with sound intellect and clear reasoning in order that he may guide himself in the right way and guard from harmful things which were created to punish the wicked.

But someone who does not want to guide himself in an intelligent manner and exposes himself to dangers - this is not trust in G-d but rather foolishness. Such a person sins in that he is acting against the will of G-d who desires that a man guard himself.

Hence, besides the inherent danger which he is exposing himself to due to failing to guard himself properly, he also actively brings punishment down upon himself for the sin which he commits. Thus, the sin itself is what brings upon him the punishment.

The type of fear and guarding of oneself which is appropriate is that which is based on the guidance of wisdom and reason. On this scripture says: "the clever man sees the evil and escapes but the fool continues through and is punished" (Mishlei 22:3).

The foolish fear is when a man wants to add protection upon protection and fear upon fear, devising precautions for his precautions in such a way that this results in neglect of Torah study and divine service.

The general principle to distinguish between the two types of fear is as our sages specified saying: "where harm is likely it is different" (Pesachim 8b).

For in a place where harm is likely and foreseeable it is proper to guard oneself. But in a place where there is no known danger one should not fear.

On similar to this the sages said: "we do not assume any defect without cause" (Chulin 56b). And "a judge need be guided only by that which his eyes see" (Bava Batra 131a). This itself is the intent of the verse we brought earlier "the clever man sees the evil and hides himself" (Mishlei 22:3), which states only about escaping from the evil that one can see not of the evil which perhaps, possibly, may occur.

This is precisely like the verse brought earlier "the lazy man says there is a lion in the way..." (Mishlei 26:13). Our sages, of blessed memory, illustrated, in successive degrees, to what extent unfounded fear can go to cause a person to refrain from good deeds. They said (Midrash Devarim Raba 8:6):

Shlomo said seven things regarding the lazy man. To illustrate:

They said to the lazy man: "Your teacher is in the city, go and learn Torah from him".

He replies: "I am afraid of the lion on the road" [Mishlei 26:13].

"Your teacher is in the neighborhood".

He replies: "I am afraid he may be between the paths" [ibid].

"He is in your building".

He replies: "if I go to him, I may find the door locked...", see there.

We learn from here that it is not the fear that causes him to be lazy, but rather the opposite, the laziness causes the fear.

Everyday experience can testify on the truth of these things as such conduct is evident and widespread among the masses of people "whose ways are folly" (Tehilim 49:13). One who thinks on this matter will find the absolute truth and knowledge will come readily to the understanding person.

We have already clarified the matter of Zeal to an extent which I deem will suffice to rouse one's heart. The wise man will become wiser and increase in understanding.

See that it is proper for the step of Zeal to follow after the step of Watchfulness. For generally a man will not be Zealous if he is not first watchful of his deeds. One who does not put to heart to be cautious in his deeds nor to contemplate the divine service and its principles, which constitutes the trait of Watchfulness as I wrote, will find it very difficult to don love and yearning for the service of G-d and to be zealous with passion before his Creator.

For such a person is still drowning in the bodily desires and running in the momentum of his habit, which distances him away from all this. But after he has opened his eyes to see his deeds, been watchful of them, made the accounting of the Mitzvot against the sins as we mentioned, it will be easy for him to turn from evil and to long for the good and be zealous in it. This is evident.

Messulat Chapter 9 Yesharim

Messilat Yesharim

Chapter 10

The trait of Cleanliness is that a man be completely clean of all bad traits and all sins. [This applies] not only for sins which are familiar and recognized but also for those to which one's heart is enticed to rationalize that it is permissible; but when we truthfully examine the matter, we find that it appeared to the person justified only because his heart was afflicted by some desire and not entirely purified of it. Therefore, it pulled him to be lenient.

But the man who was completely purified from this affliction and has been cleansed of all trace of evil which lust leaves behind it, behold his vision will be perfectly clear and his discernment will be pure. He will not be swayed by any desire. He will recognize anything which is a sin. Even for the most minuscule, he will see its evil and will distance from it. On this our Sages referred regarding the men of Sheleimut (Wholeness) who purified their deeds to such a great extent as to leave not even a stirring of evil - "the clean minded men of Jerusalem" (Sanhedrin 23a).

You can now see the distinction between the Watchful and the Clean man. Even though both are similar in their matters, the Watchful is cautious in his deeds and sees to it that he does not sin in what he already knows and which is familiar to everyone that it is a sin.

But he is still not master over himself to keep his heart from being pulled by natural lusts so that they do not sway him to rationalize that certain things are permitted regarding the things whose evil is not so well known.

For even though he strives to conquer his evil inclination and to subdue his lusts, he will not change his nature because of this. He will not be able to remove bodily lust from his heart. He will at most be able to subdue it and be governed by wisdom instead of it. But nevertheless, the darkness of the physical will inevitably do its work to entice and seduce him.

But after a man habituates himself to a great extent in Watchfulness till he has cleansed himself a first cleansing of the well known sins and has habituated himself in the service of G-d with Zeal, and love and yearning to his Creator has grown strong within him, behold the power of this habituation will distance him from physical matters and cling his intellect towards spiritual perfection, and eventually he will be able to attain perfect Cleanliness. The fire of bodily lust will extinguish from his heart due to the intensifying within him of the yearning to G-d. Then his sight will be clear and pure as

I wrote earlier, so that he will not be seduced nor deceived by the darkness of the physical and his deeds will be completely clean.

On possessing this trait David would rejoice saying: "I will wash my hands in Cleanliness and I will go around Your altar, O G-d" (Tehilim 26:6). For in truth, only he who is completely clean from any trace of sin or iniquity is fit to appear before the presence of the King, G-d. For without this, he has only to feel shame and disgrace before Him as Ezra the Scribe said: "O my G-d, I am ashamed and embarrassed to lift up my face to You [for our iniquities have increased over our head...]" (Ezra 9:6).

Certainly, it requires great work to attain Shelemut (perfection) in this trait. For the recognized and well-known sins are easy to guard from for their evil is apparent. But the scrutiny which is necessary for Cleanliness is the most difficult. For the sin is concealed by rationalizations that it is permitted as I wrote and as the sages of blessed memory said: "the sins which a man treads with his heels surround him at the time of Judgment" (Avodah Zara 18a).

Along these lines they said (Bava Batra 165a): "the majority of people are guilty of [forms of] theft, a minority in immorality, but all are guilty of the dust of slander" (i.e. traces of slander). For due to its extremely fine details, all human beings stumble in what they fail to recognize of it.

The sages of blessed memory said David was watchful and cleansed himself completely from all these things. Therefore, he would engage in war with strong trust in G-d requesting "May I pursue my enemies and overtake them, not turning back till I have destroyed them" (Tehilim 18:38), something not asked by Yehoshafat, Asa, and Chizkiyahu since they had not attained such perfect cleanliness (see Midrash Eicha Raba peticha 30).

This is what David himself said later in his words: "Reward me, O G-d, according to my righteousness, according to the purity of my hands repay me" (ibid 18:21) and "the L-rd has recompensed me according to my righteousness, according to the purity of my hands before His eyes" (ibid 18:25). This refers to this purity and cleanliness which we have mentioned. He then further said: "For by You I run upon a troop... I have pursued my enemies and overtaken them" (Tehilim 18:30). And he himself further stated: "Who will ascend upon the mountain of G-d, who will stand in His Holy place? He who has clean hands and a pure heart." (Tehilim 24:3).

Certainly, this trait is difficult to attain for man's nature is weak. His heart is easily seduced and he permits for himself things that allow for self-deception. Undoubtedly, one who has attained this trait has already reached a very high spiritual level. For he has stood in the midst of the raging battle and emerged victorious. We will now explain the details of this trait.

Messilat Yesharim

Chapter 11

The particulars of the trait of Cleanliness are very numerous. They are as all the particulars of all the 365 negative commandments. For I already mentioned that the matter of cleanliness is to be clean of all branches of the various sins.

Even though the Yetzer HaRah (evil inclination) strives to cause one to sin on every sin, nevertheless there are certain ones which a person's nature desires more. In those the Evil Inclination presents to him more rationalizations why it is permitted. Therefore, one needs to especially strengthen himself in these to a greater extent in order to vanquish his evil inclination and cleanse himself from sin. On this our sages said: "theft and forbidden relations are sins which a person's soul desires and lusts for"(Chagigah 11b).

CLEANLINESS FROM THEFT: We can observe that even though most people are not blatant thieves, literally taking with their hands the possession of their fellow and putting it in their own possessions, nevertheless, most people experience a taste of theft in their business dealings by rationalizing permission to profit through their fellow's loss. They may tell themselves: "Business is different".

Many negative commandments refer to theft such as "you shall not steal" (Shemot 20:13, "you shall not rob" Vayikra (19:13), "you shall not oppress" (ibid); "nor deny nor lie one to another" (Vayikra 19:11), "you shall not oppress one another" (Vayikra 25:14), "You shall not push back your neighbor's boundary" (Devarim 19:14). All these are divisions of the laws of theft which apply to many common business transactions and each one includes many prohibitions under it.

For it is not only the explicit and well-known deed of theft or oppression which is forbidden but rather anything which may eventually lead to such a deed and cause it is included in the prohibition. On this our sages of blessed memory said (Sanhedrin 81a): "'he did not defile the wife of his fellow' (Yechezkel 18:6) - that he did not encroach upon his fellow's trade".

Rabbi Yehuda forbade a shopkeeper to distribute roasted grain and nuts to children in order to accustom them to frequent his shop. The other Sages only permitted it because his competitors could do likewise (Bava Metzia 60a).

Our Sages of blessed memory also said: "stealing from another person is worse than stealing from Temple property, for in the former, the word 'sin' precedes the word 'betrayal' [and the opposite in the latter]….."

They likewise exempted hired workers from reciting the (Hamotzi) blessing over bread and from the last blessing of the grace after meals (Birkat Hamazon). And even in the case of reciting the Shema, they required them to pause from their work only for the first chapter (Berachoth 16b). How much more so for things that are optional. And if he transgresses this, he is considered a thief.

Aba Chilkiya did not even return the greetings of Torah scholars in order to not be idle from the work he was doing for another (Taanit 23b). Yaakov, our forefather, peace be unto him, states explicitly, "in the day heat consumed me, and the frost by night, and my sleep departed from my eyes" (Bereishis 31:40).

What will they answer then, those who occupied themselves in their own pleasures and idled from work during the time they were hired out? Or if they occupied themselves with their own affairs, each person to his own gain?

The summary of the matter: one who is hired out to his fellow for any kind of work, behold, all of his hours are sold to his employer for the workday as the Sages stated: "to hire oneself out is to sell oneself for the day" (Bava Metzia 56b). Whatever time he takes for his own pleasure, whatever it may be, is completely guilty of stealing. And if his employer does not forgive him, he is not forgiven. For the Sages already stated: "sins between man and his fellow are not atoned for on Yom Kippur until he has pacified his fellow"(Yoma 85b).

Not only that but even if one does a Mitzva (good deed) during the time of his work, it will not be considered a merit but rather a sin in his hand. For a sin cannot be considered a Mitzva. And scripture states: "[I am G-d who loves justice and] hates theft in an offering" (Isaiah 61:8). In relation to this, our Sages of blessed memory said: "one who steals a measure of wheat, mills it, bakes and recites a blessing over it, is not blessing but rather blaspheming as written 'and the robber who blesses blasphemes G-d' (Tehilim 10:3)".

Similarly, it was said: "woe to this person whose defense attorney has become his prosecutor" (Vayikra Raba 30). And like our sages of blessed memory said regarding a stolen Lulav.

This is logical for stealing an object is theft and stealing time is theft. Just like when one steals an object and does a mitzva with it, his defense attorney becomes his prosecutor. So too he who steals time and does a mitzva with it, his defense attorney also becomes his prosecutor.

The Holy One blessed be He desires only faithfulness (honesty). In regard to this scripture states: "G-d guards those who are faithful" (Tehilim 31:24), and "Open the gates and let the righteous people that keep faith enter in" (Isaiah 26:2), and "My eyes shall be on the faithful of the land so that they may dwell with Me" (Tehilim 101:6), and "are Your eyes not to faithfulness?" (Jeremiah 5:3).

Even Job testified on himself: "if my step has turned aside from the path and my heart has gone after my eyes, and if any speck has stuck to my palms" (Job 31:7). Consider this beautiful analogy in which he compared unseen theft to something which tends to stick to a person's hand (ex. flour when kneading) for even though one does not intend to go and take it and by itself it sticks to his hands, nevertheless, it remains in his hands. So too here, even though one does not go out to actually steal, it is difficult for his hands to be completely empty of theft.

In truth, all this is due to his eyes drawing his heart instead of his heart ruling over his eyes thereby not allowing them to see as pleasing the things belonging to other people. Thus, the eyes draw the heart to seek to rationalize permits (heterim) for what seems attractive and desirable to them. Therefore, Job said he did not do so. His heart did not go after his eyes. Therefore, no speck had stuck to his hands.

Consider the prohibition of Onaah (fraud/deceit). How easy it is for a person to be enticed (to find permits - SP) and to stumble in it (actual sin - SP). For it appears to him proper to strive to make his merchandise appear appealing to the eyes of people in order to make a profit from the toil of his hands; to try to speak to the prospective customer's heart in order to convince him (salesman talk). He will justify himself on all this citing: "some are industrious and profit" (Pesachim 50b) or "the hand of the diligent prospers" (Mishlei 10:4).

But if he does not meticulously examine his deeds very carefully, thorns will sprout instead of wheat. For he will transgress and stumble in the sin of Onaah (fraud) which we were warned against: "And you shall not oppress one another" (Vayikra 25:17) and our sages of blessed memory said: "even to deceive a non-Jew is forbidden" (Chulin 94a). And scripture states: "the remnant of Israel shall not do iniquity nor speak lies, neither shall a deceitful tongue be found in their mouth" (Tzefania 3:13).

Similarly, the sages said: "one may not embellish old merchandise so that it appears new" (Bava Metzia 60b).

And in (Sifri Devarim 25:16): "It is forbidden to mix fruits from another field, even if the latter are just as fresh as the former, and even if it is sold at a price of one Seah per Dinar and the mixture is worth a Dinar and a Tarsit. Even so, it is forbidden to mix them and sell the mixture for a Seah per Dinar. 'Anyone who does all these things, who commits iniquity' (Devarim 25:16) - five designations have been attributed to such people, 'unjust', 'hated', 'abominable' ('disgusting'), 'condemned', 'abhorrent'".

The Sages also stated: "if one steals from his fellow even the worth of a peruta (small coin), it is as if he takes his life from him" (Bava Kama 119a). This teaching reveals to us, the graveness of this sin even for a small amount. They further said: "the rains are withheld only because of the sin of theft" (Taanit 7b). And "for a basketful of sins, which sin prosecutes at the head of all of them? - theft" (Vayikra Raba 33:3). And "the generation of the flood had their fate sealed only because of the sin of theft" (Sanhedrin 108a).

If you ask yourself, "how is it possible for us in our business dealings to not try to convince a prospective buyer towards purchasing the merchandise and its value?"

There is a great distinction in the matter. For whatever is in order to show the prospective buyer the true value and quality of the merchandise is good and upright. But anything which is to conceal its defects is fraud (Onaah) and forbidden. This is a general principle in faithful business dealings.

I will not speak with respect to deception in the area of measurements for scripture explicitly states: "the abomination of the L-rd your G-d are all who do these" (Devarim 25:16). They further stated: "the punishment for dishonest weights and measures is worse than the punishment for illicit relations" (Bava Basra 88b) and "a wholesale dealer must wipe his measures clean once in thirty days..." (ibid 88a). Why all this? So that they do not unknowingly diminish in measure and he is not punished [for stealing from his customers due to negligence].

How much more so for the sin of taking interest, which is considered as great as denying the G-d of Israel, G-d forbid. Our sages of blessed memory commented on the verse: "he has loaned on interest; and has taken increase; shall he then live? He shall not live! [He has done all these abominations; he shall surely die; his blood shall be on him]" (Yechezkel 18:13) - "'he shall not live" refers to living in the time of the resurrection of the dead for he and his dust are abominable and detestable in the eyes of G-d' (Shemot Raba 31:6). I do not see a need to elaborate on this for its dread is already imprinted on every man of Israel.

The general principle of what has been said - just like desire for money is very great so too its stumbling blocks are very numerous. Great analysis and meticulous investigation is required in order for a person to be truly clean from them. If he has cleansed himself of them, he should know that he has already reached a high level.

For many have reached piety in various branches of piety but in the matter of hating bribes (i.e. dishonest gains), they are unable to reach the place of Shelemut (wholeness/perfection). This is what Tzofar HaNaamati told Job: "if iniquity be in your hand, put it far away, and do not permit injustice to dwell in your tents; surely then you shall lift up your face without a blemish; you shall be steadfast and shall not fear;" (Job 11:14-15).

I have spoken up to now on some of the details of one of the Mitzvot. There is no doubt that each and every mitzva also has divisions and details in a similar way. However, I will discuss only those that the majority of people habitually stumble in.

FORBIDDEN RELATIONS: Let us now discuss the topic of forbidden relations. They are also among the sins people crave and are ranked second to theft as our sages, of blessed memory, said "the majority of people are guilty of theft and a minority of illicit relations" (Bava Basra 165a).

He who wants to become completely clean of this sin will also require a laboring which is not small. For included in the prohibition is not only the act itself but even all that draws one close to it. This is explicitly stated in scripture: "do not draw near to uncover nakedness" (Vayikra 18:6).

And our Sages said: "Says the Holy One, blessed be He, 'do not say since it is forbidden for me to have intercourse with a woman, I will embrace her and be free of sin, I will caress her and be free of sin, I will kiss her and be free of sin'. Says the Holy One, blessed be He, - 'just like when a

Nazir makes a vow not to drink wine, he is also forbidden to eat grapes or raisins, diluted grape juice, or anything derived from the grape vine, so too, for a woman who is not your wife, you are forbidden to touch her in any way. Anyone who touches a woman other than his wife brings death to himself...' " (Shemot Raba 16:2).

Consider how wondrous are the words of this Midrash. For it likens this prohibition with that of the Nazir which even though the primary prohibition of Nazir is only on wine, nevertheless, the Torah forbids him all that is connected to wine. This was a lesson the Torah taught to the Sages how they should "make a fence around the Torah" so that they may use the authority granted to them to enact protections to the Torah.

For they could learn from the Nazir to prohibit all that is connected to the primary prohibition. Thus, the Torah did for this prohibition of Nazir an example of what it authorized the Sages to do for all the other Mitzvot in order to teach that this is G-d's will. So that when G-d prohibits for us some matter, we can deduce the unexplained from the explained (Nazir) to also prohibit all that draws close to the specified prohibition.

In this manner, the Sages prohibited on the matter of forbidden relations all that resembles and draws a person close to forbidden relations, however way that may be, namely, whether it be in deed, in sight, in speech, in hearing or even in thought. I will now bring you some proofs on all this from the words of the Sages of blessed memory.

In deed: namely, touching, hugging, or the like, we have already explained this earlier in the statement we brought (from Shemot Raba 16:2). There is no need to further elaborate.

In sight: Our sages, of blessed memory, said: "'from hand to hand he shall not escape from evil' (Mishlei 11:21), [this teaches] whoever counts out money from his hand to the hand of a woman in order to gaze at her, [even if he possesses Torah and good deeds like Moses our teacher,] shall not escape the punishment of Gehinom" (Berachot 61a). And: "why did the Jews of that generation require atonement? Because they fed their eyes with lewdness (Erva)" (Shab. 64b) and "Rabbi Sheshes said: 'Why does scripture enumerate the outward ornaments with the inner ones? To teach you: Whoever looks upon a woman's little finger is as though he gazed upon her private parts" (ibid).

They further taught: "'you shall keep yourself from every evil thing' (Devarim 23:10) [this teaches] that one should not look intently at a beautiful woman, even if she be unmarried, or at a married woman even if she be ugly" (Avodah Zara 20b).

In speech: it was taught explicitly: "one who speaks excessively to a woman brings evil upon himself" (Avot 2:5).

In hearing: it was taught: "a woman's voice is Erva (sexual incitement)" (Berachot 24a).

Furthermore, regarding the matter of lewdness of the mouth and the ear, namely, speaking words of lewdness or listening to them, our sages already "screamed like cranes" saying (on the verse): "'there shall not be any indecent (Erva) thing among you' (Devarim 23:15) - this refers to lewdness of speech" (Yerushalmi Teruma 1:6).

They further said (Shabbat 33a): "Due to the sin of obscene speech, new troubles arise and the young men of Israel die" (Isaiah 9:16)

And "whoever utters obscene language, Gehinom is made deep for him [as it is said, A deep pit is for the mouth that speaks perversity] (Mishlei 22:14)

And further: "All know for what purpose a bride enters the bridal canopy, yet against whoever speaks obscenely thereof, even if a decree of seventy years of good had been sealed for him, it is reversed for evil" (Shabbat 33a).

They further said: "Even the light talk between a man and his wife is declared to a person in the time of his Judgment" (Chagigah 5b).

And regarding listening to obscenities it is likewise taught: "even one who listens and remains silent, as written '[The mouth of strange women is like a deep pit;] the one abhorred by G-d will fall therein'" (Shabbat 33a).

This demonstrates to you that all the senses must be be clean of lewdness and anything related to it.

If a man will foolishly claim to you: "that which the sages said regarding obscene language is only in order to frighten and distance a person from sin, and it is meant only for those whose blood is boiling, namely, when he speaks of these things, he becomes aroused to lust. But one who just says it in a joking manner, it is not significant and of no concern."

Answer him that his words are those of the evil inclination. For the Sages brought their proofs from an explicit verse in scripture: "As a punishment for obscenity, troubles multiply, cruel decrees are proclaimed afresh, the youths of Israel die... for every one is a flatterer and slanderer, and every mouth speaks obscenities" (Isaiah 9:16). This verse mentions neither idol worship nor illicit relations nor murder but flattery, slander, and obscene speech. All of which are sins of the mouth in speech. And on these the decree went forth: "the youths of Israel die and the fatherless and widows cry out and are not answered... neither shall He have compassion."

Rather, the truth is as the words of our sages, of blessed memory, that uttering obscene words is in fact lewdness of speech. It is an aspect of lewdness and falls under the same prohibition as all other matters of lewdness except for the actual act of illicit relations. Even though it does not incur the heavenly punishment of Karet (cutting off of the soul) or death by Beit Din (like the act of illicit relations), they are nevertheless prohibited in and of themselves. This is besides being things which lead to and draw one to the primary prohibition itself, similar to the case of the Nazir in the Midrash we brought earlier.

Regarding "thought" our Sages already mentioned in the beginning of our Beraitha: "'you shall keep yourself from every evil thing' (Devarim 23:10) - From here R. Pinchas b. Yair said that a person should not have [impure] thoughts in his heart, and thus bring himself to have impurity at night" (Ketubot 46a). They further said: "thoughts of sin are worse than the sin itself" (Yoma 29a) and scripture says explicitly: "evil thoughts are an abomination to G-d" (Mishlei 15:26).

We have spoken on two severe sins which people are near to stumble in their branches due to the multitude of these branches and due to the great inclination of a man's heart towards them owing to lusting for them.

FORBIDDEN FOODS: The sin which ranks third after theft and forbidden relations in respect to desire is that of forbidden foods, whether in unkosher meat itself, mixtures of it, meat and milk, blood, food cooked by gentiles, utensils used by gentiles, their wine libations and plain wine. For all these, cleanliness in them requires great meticulousness and strengthening oneself. For there is lust in the heart for good foods and there is financial loss incurred in the prohibitions of mixtures or the like.

Their details are numerous, all being familiar laws which are explained in the books of halachic rulings. One who is lenient in them when the sages ruled that one must be stringent is only destroying his soul as the sages said in the Sifra (parsha Shmini): "'do not defile yourselves, becoming Tamei (spiritual contaminated) with them' (Vayikra 11:43) if you defile yourself in them you will in the end become Tamei in them".

This is because the forbidden foods bring in Tuma (spiritual contamination) in a person's heart and soul so that the holiness of G-d, blessed be He, departs and withdraws from him. This is also what they stated (Yoma 39a): "'becoming defiled with them' (Vayikra 11:43) - read not ve-nitmetem [that you will be defiled], but ve-nitamtem [that you will become dull-hearted]".

For sin dulls a man's heart, causing to depart from him true knowledge and the spirit of wisdom which the Holy One, blessed be He, bestows to the pious, as written "for G-d grants wisdom" (Mishlei 2:6). Thus, he is left animal-like and material, sunk in the coarseness of this world.

The forbidden foods are worse in this regard than all other sins since they literally enter a person's body and become flesh of his flesh. And in order to teach us that it is not only the unkosher animals and creatures that contain this Tuma (spiritual contamination) but rather even the disqualified Kosher animals themselves (Treifot) also. Scripture says: "to distinguish between the impure (Tamei) and the pure (Tahor)" (Vayikra 11:47), and the explanation received by our Rabbis of blessed memory:

"It is not necessary to teach us about the distinction between a donkey and a cow. Why then does scripture state: 'between the impure and the pure'? [Answer:] Rather it is referring to between impure to you and pure to you, namely, between a kosher animal whose majority of the windpipe was cut to one where only half of its windpipe was cut. And how much difference is there between a majority and a half? - one hair's breadth" (Sifra Shemini ch.12).

The reason they concluded their teaching with the words "and how much difference between a majority, etc." is in order to demonstrate how wondrous is the power of the Mitzva whereby a mere hair's breadth separates between Tuma (impure) and Tahara (pure).

Behold, any person with a brain in his head will consider forbidden food as poison or like food which has been mixed with poison. For behold if such a case would present itself would he be lenient on himself and eat from such food?

If there were reason to suspect, even the slightest one, would he be lenient? Certainly, he would not. And if he were lenient, people would consider him to be a complete fool!

The prohibition in the food, as we explained, is literally a poison to the heart and soul. If so, then who among the sensible will be lenient in a situation where there is suspicion of prohibition in the food? On this it is written "and put a knife into your mouth, if you are a person given to appetite" (Mishlei 23:2).

Let us now speak on the common sins which arise from interaction with people and being among them such as oppression of speech, shaming, misleading the blind through [bad] advice, tale-bearing, hating, taking revenge, taking oaths, lying and desecrating G-d's Name. For who can say: "I am clean of them. I have become pure from sinning in them"? For their branches are exceedingly numerous and fine so that guarding from them requires great effort.

WORDS THAT HURT: Included in the sin of oppression of speech (Ona'as Devarim) is to say to someone, in private, something [implicit] which may cause him shame. All the more so, to say something explicit which causes him shame or to do to him an act which causes him shame.

This is what our sages said: "if he were a Baal Teshuva (penitent), do not say to him 'remember your former deeds...' if sickness befalls him do not say to him in the way the friends of Job said: "Remember, please, who ever perished, being innocent?" (Job 4:7). If traveling merchants ask you for grain, do not tell them 'go to such and such who sells grain', and you know that he never sold grain in his life" (Bava Metzia 58b).

Our sages of blessed memory already said "verbal oppression is more severe than monetary oppression..." (ibid). This is even more so, if the shaming is done in public as we learned explicitly: "one who whitens his neighbor's face (shames him) publicly has no portion in the World to Come" (Avot 5:11), and Rabbi Chisda taught (Bava Metzia 59a): "all the gates [of prayer] were locked except the gates of [the cries of] verbal oppression". Rabbi Eliezer taught "for every sin, the Holy One, blessed be He, exacts payment through a messenger except for the sin of verbal oppression".

And they taught "for three sins the Pargud (heavenly curtain) is never closed....", and one of those is verbal oppression. Even for the sake of performing a mitzva whereby scripture says: "you shall surely rebuke your neighbor" (Vayikra 19:14), and our sages, of blessed memory, said: "One might assume [this to be obligatory] even to the extent that his face whitened, therefore the verse continues: 'but do not bear sin because of him' " (Erchin 16b).

From all these statements, you can see just how far the branches of this sin spread out and just how severe is its punishment.

GIVING MISLEADING ADVICE: Regarding giving [misleading] advice, we were taught in Torat Kohanim (2:14): "'you shall not put a stumbling block before the blind' (Vayikra 19:14), i.e. before one who is blind in some matter. [For example,] if one asks you: 'is the daughter of so and so permitted to marry a Kohen?' Do not answer him 'she is permitted' when she is not. If he consulted you for advice, do not give him an advice which is not suitable to him... Do not say to him 'sell your house and buy a donkey', while in truth you intend to circumvent him and buy it from him. Perhaps you will say: "I am giving him a good advice" - this is a [hidden] matter given over to thought, thus the verse warns "you shall fear your G-d" (who knows your thoughts).

Hence, we learn that whether in a matter where one may possibly have a vested interest or none at all, he is obligated to establish the person coming to him for advice on the pure and clear truth.

You can observe that the Torah had a full grasp of the deceivers' thinking. For we are not speaking here of fools whose evil advice is apparent and noticeable. But rather with wise deceivers, who give advice to their neighbor which on the surface appears to truly be beneficial to his neighbor, but in the end of the matter it is not to his benefit but rather to his detriment, benefiting only the advisor. Therefore, they said: "perhaps you will say: 'I am giving him a good advice'... this is a hidden matter of thought... ['you shall fear your G-d']".

Oh, to what extent do people stumble in these sins every day, called and impelled by the force of desire for profit! The severity of their punishment has already been revealed in scripture: "cursed be he who misleads a blind man on the road" (Devarim 27:18).

The obligation of the upright man when someone comes to him for advice is to counsel him what he himself would have done in a similar situation, without looking at any purpose whatsoever, distant or immediate, other than the benefit of the person asking advice.

And if it occurs that he anticipates some loss to himself as a result of this advice, then if he is able to admonish the advisee directly, he should do so. Otherwise, he should withdraw from the matter and not give any advice. In any case, he must not give an advice whose purpose is other than the benefit of the advisee, unless the intent of the advisee is evil, in which case it is certainly a mitzva to deceive him. And scripture already said: "but with a crooked one, You deal crookedly" (Tehilim 18:27), and the story of Chushai the Archite demonstrates it.

SLANDER AND EVIL SPEECH: Tale-bearing and slander – it is severity is already known, as are its great branches for they are exceedingly numerous. Their extent are such that our Sages of blessed memory said, as I quoted earlier, "all stumble in the dust of slander" (Bava Basra 165a).

They taught (Erchin 15b): "What is [the dust of] slander? [Answer:] For instance to say 'where else should there be fire if not in the house of so-and-so?' (implying that there is always meat and fish there)". Or to praise a person before one who hates him. Likewise, for all similar cases, even though they may appear like insignificant words, far removed from tale-bearing, behold, in truth, they are of the "dust" of slander.

The general principle is that the evil inclination has many ways. But any words which could potentially lead to damage or shame to one's fellow whether the words are uttered in his presence or not is included in the sin of evil speech, which is hated and despised before G-d, and which the sages said "whoever speaks evil speech is as if he denied G-d" (Erchin 15b) and scripture says: "He who slanders his neighbor in secret, I will cut him down" (Tehilim 101:5).

HATRED AND VENGEANCE: Hatred and vengeance are likewise exceedingly difficult for the mocked heart of human beings to escape from. For a human being strongly feels insults and he experiences great pain therein. Revenge is then sweeter to him than honey for it alone is his peace.

Therefore for one to have the strength to relinquish what his nature impels him to and to overlook the wronging, not hating the one who ignited hatred in his heart, not exacting vengeance when he has the opportunity to do so nor bearing a grudge against him, but rather to forget the whole incident and remove it from his heart as if it had never happened - he is mighty and courageous.

Such forbearance is easy only to the ministering angels who do not have among them these traits, but not to human beings "who dwell in houses of clay, whose foundation is in the dust" (Job 4:19). But it is a decree of the King, and the scriptural verses state in explicit and clear language, requiring no explanation: "you shall not hate your brother in your heart" (Vayikra 19:17), "you shall not take vengeance nor bear a grudge against the members of your people" (Vayikra 19:18).

The explanation of taking vengeance and bearing a grudge is known.

Vengeance is to refrain from doing good to someone who kept good from him or who committed wrong to him.

Bearing a grudge is to remind the wrongdoer some reminder of the wrong he committed to him while he is doing good to him.

But the Yetzer (evil inclination) advances and stokes the heart, seeking constantly to leave at least some trace or remembrance of the wrong. If he is unsuccessful in leaving a large remembrance, he will attempt to leave a small remembrance. For instance, he will say to a person: "if you want to give this person that which he did not want to give you when you were in need, at least do not give it with a pleasant facial expression". Or "if you do not want to hurt him at least do not do to him a great favor or help him greatly." Or "even if you want to help him greatly, at least do not do so in his presence or do not resume associating with him and continuing your friendship with him. If you forgave him and do not show yourself as an enemy, this is enough". Or, "even if you want to continue being his friend, at least do not show him so much affection as before".

All such arguments are among the diligent efforts of the Yetzer with which he strives to entice the hearts of people. The Torah therefore came and stated a general principle which includes everything: "you shall love your neighbor as yourself" (Vayikra 19:18) - "as yourself", with no difference whatsoever, "as yourself" without any distinction, without strategies and ploys, literally "as yourself".

OATHS: Regarding Oaths, even though normally anyone who is not of the boorish type, guards himself from uttering G-d's Name in vain, and surely more so for Oaths, nevertheless there are some small offshoots of this sin which although they are not among the most severe sins, nevertheless, it is proper for one who wants to be Clean to guard himself from them.

This is what the sages said in the Talmud (Shavuot 36a):"R. Eleazar said: 'No' is an oath; 'Yes' is an oath... Said Raba: But only if he said, 'No! No!' twice; or he said, 'Yes! Yes!' twice".

Similarly, they said (Bava Metzia 49a): "[What is taught by the verse (Vayikra 19:36):] 'A just Hin [shall you have', surely 'Hin' is included in 'Ephah'?] [Answer] it is to teach you that your 'yes' [hen] should be just and your 'no' should be just! [Abaye said: That means that one must not speak one thing with the mouth and another with the heart]".

LYING: Lying is also an evil disease that has spread out far among people. There are various levels therein.

There are some people whose profession is lying. Namely, those people who go around and make up complete lies in order to increase social conversation or to be considered among the intelligent and knowledgeable. On this type it is written "lying lips are an abomination to G-d" (Mishlei 12:22). And also "your lips speak lies, your tongue mutters perverseness" (Isaiah 59:3). Our sages, of blessed memory, have already pronounced their judgment: "four classes of people do not receive the divine presence" (Sanhedrin 103a, Sota 42a), and one of these is the class of liars.

There are other liars close to the first group in level [of lying] but not exactly like them. Namely, those who lie in their reports and statements. These peoples' profession is not to go around and make up stories and deeds that never were nor will be. But when they come to tell over something, they mix in whatever lies they happen to think of. They habituate in this until it becomes part of their nature. These are the liars whose word is impossible to believe. This is as what our sages, of blessed memory, said: "it is the penalty of a liar, that even when he tells the truth, he is not listened to" (Sanhedrin 89b). For this evil has ingrained itself in their nature such that their words are unable to leave their mouths free of falsehood. It is about this that the prophet grieved and said: "they have taught their tongue to speak lies, they weary themselves to commit iniquity" (Yirmiya 9:4).

There are others still whose illness is milder than that of the first [two]. Namely, those who are not so entrenched in falsehood, but are not concerned to distance from it. They will lie when the opportunity presents itself, often in a joking manner or the like without evil intent.

But the wisest of men (Shlomo) has taught us that all of this is contrary to the will of the Creator, blessed be He, and the attributes of His pious ones as written: "the righteous man hates a false word" (Mishlei 13:5). This is also what the Torah commands us: "keep far from a false matter" (Shemot 23:7). Notice that the verse did not say "guard against falsehood" but rather "keep far from a false matter", to rouse us on the great extent one must distance and flee far away from falsehood, as scripture says: "The remnant of Israel shall not do iniquity nor speak lies, and a deceitful tongue shall not be found in their mouths" (Tzefania 3:13).

And our sages, of blessed memory, said: "the seal of the Holy One, blessed be He, is truth" (Shab.55a). If "truth" is what the Holy One, blessed be He, selected as His seal, then undoubtedly, how great of an abomination must its opposite be to Him!

The Holy One blessed be He exhorted us greatly on speaking the truth, such as: "let each man speak the truth to his neighbor" (Zech.8:16). And "in mercy the throne shall be established; and he shall sit upon it in Truth" (Isaiah 16:5). And "for He said, surely they are My people, sons that will not lie" (Isaiah 63:8) - which teaches you that the one depends on the other.

And "[I have returned to Zion, and will dwell in the midst of Jerusalem:] and Jerusalem shall be called the City of Truth" (Zecharia 8:3) - to magnify its importance. And our sages of blessed memory said (Makot 24a): "'who speaks truth in his heart' (Tehilim 15:2), like Rav Safra..." To teach you just how far-reaching the obligation of truth extends.

The sages forbade a Torah scholar to alter his word except for three things.

Truth is one of the pillars upon which the world stands (Avot 1:18). Therefore, one who speaks falsehood is as if he removes the foundation of the world, and conversely, one who is scrupulous on the truth, it is as if he upholds the foundation of the world.

Our sages of blessed memory reported (Sanhedrin 97a) of a certain town whose inhabitants were so heedful of truth that the angel of death had no dominion over them. But because the wife of a certain Rabbi changed her word, even though her intention was good, the angel of death began to prevail over them. They expelled her from there due to this and their former tranquility was restored.

There is no need to elaborate further on this topic for reason dictates this and knowledge forces it.

PROFANATION OF G-D's NAME (Chilul Ha-shem): The Branches of the sin of "profanation of [G-d's] Name" (Chillul Ha-shem) are also numerous and great. For a person must be exceedingly concerned of his Master's honor. In everything he does, he must look and contemplate exceedingly that there will not come out of this something which may cause a profanation of the honor of Heaven, G-d forbid.

We have learned: "whether one has acted in error or whether he has acted deliberately it is all one and the same where the result is the desecration of G-d's Name" (Avot 4:4).

Our sages, of blessed memory, taught: "What constitutes profanation of the Name? Rav said: If, for example, I were to take meat from the butcher and not pay him at once... Rabbi Yochanan said: In my case [it is a profanation if] I walk four cubits without Torah and Tefillin." (Yoma 86a).

The explanation of the matter is that every person according to his level and according to what he is considered in the eyes of his generation, must be mindful to not do something which is not befitting of someone like him. The greater his importance and wisdom, the greater he needs to increase watchfulness and meticulousness in the divine service. If he fails to do so, behold, the Name of Heaven will be profaned through him, G-d forbid. For it is an honor to the Torah, that one who increases study in it, should also increase uprightness and refinement of character traits. Any lacking in this among those who increase study in the Torah brings disgrace to the study itself. This is, G-d forbid, a profanation of G-d's Name, blessed be He, who gave us His holy Torah and commanded us to toil in it order to achieve our perfection through it.

SABBATH AND HOLIDAY OBSERVANCE: Guarding of the Sabbath and Holiday observance is also severe for the laws are very numerous. Thus our sages said: "this is a great law of the Sabbath" (Shab.12a).

Even matters of Shevut (Resting), despite that they are Rabbinical, are nevertheless important principles as the Sages said: "Never let [the principle] of Shevut (Rest) be light in your eyes. For the laying on of the hands [on a sacrifice for a Festival-day] is [prohibited] only on account of Shevut, yet the greatest men of the age debated therein" (Chagigah 16b).

The details of these laws according to their differences are explained by the Halachic deciders (Poskim) in their books. All of these details are equal for all us with respect to their obligation and requisite watchfulness. That which is difficult on the masses to guard is abstaining from business occupation and conversation. This prohibition is stated in the words of the prophet (Isaiah 58:13): "if you honor it, abstaining from your own ways, not pursuing your affairs and speaking words about them". The general principle is that whatever is forbidden to do on the Sabbath is forbidden to strive after or mention verbally.

Hence, our Sages forbade one to examine his property to see what is needed for tomorrow (Shab.150a) or to walk to the border of the province in order to leave quickly after nightfall for the bathhouse (Eruvin 39a). And the sages forbid one to say "I will do such and such tomorrow", "or such and such merchandise I will buy tomorrow" (ibid), or the like.

Thus far I have spoken on some of the mitzvot which we see most people stumble in. From these we can apply what we learned to all other negative precepts. For there is no Torah prohibition which does not contain branches and details, some more severe, some less. One who aspires to Cleanliness must be clean and pure in all of them.

Our sages already stated (Shir HaShirim Raba 6:6): "'your teeth are like a flock of ewes [not one among them has lost its young]' - just as an ewe is modest [so too were the Israelites modest and virtuous in the war with Midian], Rav Huna said in the name of Rav Acha: 'not one of them put on the head Tefilin before the arm Tefilin. For if one among them had done so, Moshe would not have praised them and they would not have come out of that war in peace".

As stated: "one who speaks between 'Yishtabach' and 'Yotzer' has a sin on his hand, and he leaves from the battlefield on account of this" (Shulchan Aruch O.C. 51:4).

So you see just how far the meticulousness and Cleanliness must be truly attained in one's deeds.

CLEANLINESS IN CHARACTER TRAITS: Just like Cleanliness is needed [to acquire] for the deeds, so too cleanliness is needed for the character traits. One can almost say that Cleanliness in character traits is more difficult to acquire than in the deeds. For human nature influences the traits more than it does in the deeds and one's natural temperament and disposition can either greatly aid or greatly impede in this area. Thus, any war waged against one's nature becomes a raging battle. This is what our sages referred to saying: "who is mighty? He who conquers his inclination (Yetzer)" (Avot 4:1).

The character traits are very numerous. Just like there are many different actions that a man can do in the world, so too there are [many] character traits, for a man's actions are drawn after them.

However, just like we discussed only those Mitzvot which were most necessary, namely, those which people habitually stumble in, so too regarding the character traits, we will discuss the primary traits in greater detail because of our habituation in them. These are arrogance, anger, jealousy, and lust.

These are all evil traits whose evil is recognized and well-known. No proof is necessary to demonstrate this, for they are both evil in themselves and evil in their consequences. They are all outside the realm of intellect and wisdom and each one of them is sufficient by itself to lead a person to severe sins.

On arrogance, scripture explicitly warns saying: "then your heart will grow haughty, and you will forget the L-rd, your G-d" (Devarim 8:14).

On anger, our sages of blessed memory said (Shab.105b, Zohar 3:179): "anyone who becomes angry should be regarded in your eyes as one who worships idols".

On jealousy and lust, we learned explicitly: "jealousy, lust, and honor remove a person out of the world" (Avot 4:21).

The in-depth study necessary in relation to them must be such that one escapes from them and all of their branches for they are one and all as "degenerate branches of a strange vine"(Yirmiyahu 2:21). Let us speak on each of them one at a time.

ARROGANCE: Generally, the matter of arrogance is that a man ascribes importance to himself on himself and imagines that he is worthy of praise.

This could grow out of many different reasons. Some people consider themselves of high intelligence. Some consider themselves handsome. Some consider themselves important or great or wise. The general principle of the matter: if a person thinks he possesses any of the good things of the world, he is in immediate danger of falling in this pit of arrogance.

But, after a person has fixed in his heart that he is important and praiseworthy, the consequences of this thought will not be only one thing. Rather, many different outgrowths will result out of this, some even contradictory to each other. But they all stem from one cause and direct to the same end.

Behold, there is one type of arrogant person who will convince himself that since he is praiseworthy and uniquely distinguished due to his qualities, as he imagines, it is thus proper that he conduct himself also in a uniquely distinguished and slow manner. Whether in his walking or sitting down or getting up, or whether in his speech or gestures or whether in all of his deeds, he will walk only in a very slow manner, toe touching heel. He will sit only in a reclining manner. He will get up only slowly, like a snake.

He will not speak to everyone but rather only to the honorable people, and even with them, he will utter only short phrases like the Terafim. In all the rest of his actions, in his movements, his deeds, his eating and drinking, his clothing, and in all of his other actions – he will conduct himself with great heaviness as if all of his flesh were lead and his bones were made of stone or sand.

There is another type of arrogant person who thinks that since he is worthy of praise and possesses many superior virtues, therefore he must quake the earth, so that everyone will tremble before him. He will not consent that people should penetrate through to speak to him nor ask from him something. And if they dare ascend up to him, he will confound them with his voice, and baffle them with the breath of his lips by answering them harshly. His face appears grumpy at all times.

There is another arrogant person who thinks in his heart that he is already so great and distinguished that honor is inseparable from him and he has no need for it whatsoever. To show this to others, he performs deeds like the humble all the while announcing his traits, trying to appear exceedingly lowly and absolutely humble. But his heart swells up within him saying: "I am so exalted and so honorable that I no longer have any need for honor. I may as well forego it for it is already abundant within me".

One may find another arrogant person who wants to be very renowned for his qualities and unique in his ways to the point where it is not enough for him to be praised by the whole world for the virtues, he thinks he has. Rather he wants that they praise him even more for being the humblest of the humble. Hence, this person prides himself on his humility and desires honor for appearing to flee from it. This arrogant person will set his place among those of much lower status than himself or among the disgraceful men thinking that through this he displays absolute humility. He does not wish for any titles of greatness and refuses all praise, all the while saying to himself: "there is no wiser and humbler person than me in the whole world".

Such arrogant people although they may appear to be humble, nevertheless there are no lack of stumbling blocks which, without their knowledge, reveal their arrogance like the flame which bursts forth between shards. Our sages of blessed memory have already made an analogy on this: "this is like a house full of straw. The walls had cracks through which the straw entered. After some days, the straw inside the cracks began to emerge outside. Thus, everyone realized that the house was full of straw" (Bamidbar Rabba 18:17).

So too here, these arrogant men are unable to hide themselves at all times. Their evil thoughts will show through their acts. Their ways are of false humility and deceitful lowliness.

One may find other arrogant people whose arrogance remains buried in their hearts. They will not express it in deed but they will think in their hearts that they are already great sages, who know things to their true depth and that not many will ever attain wisdom like them. Therefore, they will not pay heed to the words of others thinking that whatever is difficult for them to understand will not be easy for others. Likewise, they will think that what their mind dictates is so clear and evident to them that there is no need to consider the views of those who disagree with them, neither the views of the early sages or the later ones. They have no doubt on their reasoning.

All these aforementioned cases stem from arrogance, which backtracks the wise, rendering them foolish, depraving the hearts of the highest in wisdom.

How much more so for the disciples [of the sages] who did not sufficiently study from the wise such that their eyes are almost open and they already deem themselves equal to the wisest of the wise.

On all of them it is written "a proud heart is an abomination to G-d" (Mishlei 16:5). One who wants to reach the trait of Cleanliness must cleanse himself of all of them. He must know and understand that arrogance is literally blindness whereby a man's intellect fails to see his own deficiencies and recognize his own lowliness.

For if a man were capable of seeing and perceiving the truth, he would withdraw and distance far away from all these evil and crooked ways. We will discuss this more, with G-d's help, when we arrive at the trait of Humility, which, due to the great difficulty in attaining it, was placed among the last of the traits in the ladder of Rabbi Pinchas ben Yair.

ANGER: Let us now discuss anger. There is an anger-prone person about which our sages said: "whoever gets angry is as if he worships idols" (Zohar Korach daf 179, Rambam Deos 2:3, Shab.105b). This person gets angry on anything that is done against his will. He becomes filled with wrath till his heart is no longer with him and his judgment is lost.

A man like this would suffice to destroy the whole world if he had the ability. For the intellect does not rule over him in the least. He has literally lost his reason just like all the predatory beasts. On him it is written: "you who tears his soul in his anger; shall the earth become forsaken because of you?" (Job 18:4). Certainly, he can easily transgress any sort of sin in the world to which his rage leads him, for he has no other power moving him other than his anger and will go wherever it takes him.

There is another angry type far from this. This person's wrath is not kindled for every thing, small or big, which does not happen according to his will. But when his threshold of anger is reached, he will erupt in great fury. This is what our sages, of blessed memory, said: "difficult to anger and difficult to appease" (Avot 5:11). This type is also certainly very evil, for great damage may happen through him during his [eruption] of anger, and he will no longer be able to straighten what he has made crooked.

There is another angry type less severe than the previous. He does not come to anger easily, and even if his anger is triggered, it will only be a small anger and he will not stray out of the ways of reason. But he still harbors his angry feeling. This man is less likely to cause harm than the previous types but nevertheless he certainly has not reached Cleanliness, for even Watchfulness he has not yet reached since as long as anger marks an impression over him, he has not gone out of the category of "a person of anger".

There is another type even less than this. This person is difficult to anger and his anger does not damage and destroy. Rather, it is a small anger. How long does his anger last? It lasts only an instant and not more. From the time his anger's natural stirring is roused till the time his understanding rises up against it. This is what our sages, of blessed memory, referred to saying: "difficult to anger and easy to appease". Behold, certainly this is a good portion, for it is human nature to be roused to anger and if one overpowers it so that even at the moment of anger itself, it will not ignite much and he overcomes it so that even this small amount of anger does not linger within him for a long time, rather it quickly passes and goes away - he is certainly worthy of praise.

Our sages of blessed memory said (Chullin 89a):"'who hangs the earth on nothing (belima)' (Iyov 26:7) - [the earth endures on the merit of] one who restrains (bolem) his mouth during a dispute". Namely, his nature has roused him to anger and through strengthening himself over it, he restrains his tongue.

The level of Hillel the Elder, however, was above all of these for he was not upset for anything whatsoever and not even a stirring of anger roused within him. This is certainly one who is absolutely Clean of anger.

Our sages of blessed memory warned us to not get angry even for the sake of a mitzva (see Shab.34a, 105b), not even a teacher with his student or a father with his son. This is not to say he should not chastise them, rather he should surely chastise them, just not out of anger, but rather, with no other purpose than guiding them along the right path. Any anger that he shows to them should be only of the face not anger of the heart. Shlomo said: "Be not quick in your spirit to be angry [for anger rests in the heart of fools]" (Kohelet 7:9) and it is written "For anger slays the fool" (Iyov 5:2), and our sages of blessed memory said: "in three ways a man is recognized: through his cup, through his wallet and through his anger" (Eruvin 65b).

JEALOUSY: Jealousy also is nothing but lack of understanding and foolishness. For the jealous person gains nothing for himself nor does he cause any loss to the person he is jealous of. He only causes loss to himself as the verse we mentioned states "jealousy slays the foolish" (Iyov 5:2).

There are those whose folly has grown so great that if he sees some good by his fellow, he will rot inside. He worries and suffers so much that even the good things he has do not give him any enjoyment due to the pain of what he sees in his fellow's hands. This is what the wise man said: "jealousy is the rot of the bones"(Mishlei 14:30).

There are other types who do not suffer and pain so much by jealousy. But nevertheless, feel some suffering or at least some cooling of spirit when seeing someone rising to some higher position unless it is one of their beloved and closest friends. All the more so will he feel [suffering] if he is not so fond of the person, and further still if it is some stranger from a foreign land.

It is possible that you will see them say things as if they were happy and thankful for his good fortune but their hearts feel bad inside them. This is something that happens commonly to most people. For even though they may not be overcome by jealousy (like the first group), nevertheless they are still not completely Clean of it. This especially happens if it is someone in his own trade which succeeds for "every craftsman hates his fellow [craftsman]" (Bereishis Raba 19:2), and all the more so still if that fellow is more successful than himself.

But if they would know and understand that "no man can touch what is designated for his fellow even a hair's breadth" (Yoma 38b), and that everything is from G-d according to His wondrous judgment and unfathomable wisdom, they would have no reason whatsoever to feel pained by the good fortune of their neighbors.

This is what the prophet foretells to us on the future era, that the Holy One, blessed be He, will first remove this ugly trait from our hearts in order for the good of Israel to be perfect. At that time no one will feel pain in the good of another and also there will be no need for a successful person to conceal himself and his matters due to the jealousy of others.

This is what the prophet says: "And the envy of Ephraim shall cease, and the adversaries of Judah shall be cut off; Ephraim shall not envy Judah..." (Isaiah 11:13). This is the peace and contentment among the ministering angels who all rejoice in their service, each in his place, no one feeling any jealousy whatsoever on the other, for they all know the full truth, delighting on the good in their hands and happy with their lot.

LUST FOR WEALTH AND HONOR: You will observe that the sisters of jealousy are desire and lust. This is what wearies a man's heart until the day of his death as our sages said: "no man dies with half of his lusts attained"(Kohelet Raba 1:13).

The root of Lust splits to two main branches. The first is lust for money and the second is lust for honor, both are very evil and bring on a man many evil consequences.

LUST FOR MONEY: It is the lust for money which binds a man in the shackles of this world, harnessing thick ropes of labor and preoccupation upon his arms, as scripture says "one who loves money will never be satiated with money" (Kohelet 5:9).

It is what takes a person away from the service of G-d, for so many prayers are lost and so many mitzvot are neglected due to excessive preoccupation and much laboring after profit. How much more so regarding Torah study as our sages said (Eruvin 55a): "'it is not over the sea' (Devarim 30:13) - with those who travel over the seas for business".

Likewise, we learned: "nor do all who engage in much business become wise" (Avot 2:5). The lust for money exposes him to many dangers and weakens his strength with many worries, even after he has attained a great amount as we learned: "one who increases possessions, increases worry" (Avot 2:7). It is lust for money which leads him many times to transgress the mitzvot of the Torah and even the natural precepts of reason.

LUST FOR HONOR: Greater than this is the lust for honor. For it was already possible for a man to conquer his Yetzer (evil inclination) for money and the other pleasures, but honor is the [ultimate] difficulty. For it is impossible for him to bear and to see himself inferior to his peers. On this many have stumbled and been lost.

Behold, Yerovam ben Nevat lost his portion in the World to Come only due to honor. This is what our sages said: "the Holy One blessed be He seized him by his garment and said to him: 'repent and you and I and the son of Yishai (David) will stroll together in the Garden of Eden'. Yeravam asked: 'who will be at the head?' G-d replied: 'the son of Yishai will be at the head'. Yeravam replied: 'if so, I don't want'."

What caused the destruction of Korach and his assembly? Only honor as scripture states explicitly: "do you also seek the priesthood?" (Bamidbar 16:10). Our sages told us that all this grew out of Korach's seeing Elitzafan ben Uziel promoted to head of the tribe, and he wanted to be head in his place (Bamidbar Rabbah 18:2).

And according to our sages of blessed memory, what caused the spies to utter evil speech on the land leading to their death and the death of an entire generation. They feared that others will take over their position when they enter Israel thereby diminishing their honor, namely that they will no longer be chiefs over Israel (Zohar Bamidbar 158a).

What caused Shaul to begin to ambush David? Only honor as written: "And the women sang to one another as they celebrated: 'Saul has struck down his thousands, and David his tens of thousands'... And Saul eyed David from that day on" (Shmuel 18:7-9).

What caused Yoav to kill Amasa? Only honor. For David said to him: "you will be commander of the army before me all the days [instead of Yoav]" (Shmuel II 19:14).

The general principle: honor is what pushes a man's heart more powerfully than every other lust and desire in the world. Without this, a man would suffice to eat whatever he could, to wear whatever cover his nakedness, and to dwell in a house which shelters him from harm. His livelihood would be easy on him and he would not feel any need whatsoever to strain himself to attain wealth.

But since he cannot bear to see himself lower and lesser than his peers, he puts himself squarely under the thickness of the beam. Thus, there is no end to all his labor. Therefore, our Teachers, of blessed memory, taught us "jealousy, lust, and honor remove a person from the world" (Avot 4:21), and warned us: "do not seek greatness for yourself, and do not lust for honor" (Avot 6:5).

How many people starve themselves? How many people stoop themselves low to take their sustenance from charity rather than engage in a livelihood which is not honorable in their eyes fearing diminishing of their honor?! Is there no greater folly than this?!

They prefer idleness which brings to mental illness, to immorality (Kesuvos 59b), to theft (Shab.33a) and to all root sins, rather than lower their stature and detract their imaginary honor.

However, our sages of blessed memory, who always instructed us and guided us on the paths of truth said: "love work and hate Rabanut" (Avot 1:10), and further "flay carcasses in the marketplace and earn wages and do not say, 'I am an important man, I am a Kohen, [and it is beneath my dignity]'." (Pesachim 113a), and further "one should always hire himself out to work which is strange to him rather than be dependent [on the help] of others" (Bava Basra 110a).

FINAL WORDS: The general principle: the desire for honor is one of the biggest stumbling blocks before a man and it is impossible to be a faithful servant to his Master all the time that he is concerned for his own honor. For then he will need to detract from the honor of heaven due to this foolishness. This is what King David, peace be unto him, said: "I shall be even less than this still and be low in my own sight" (Shmuel II 6:22).

True honor is nothing but true knowledge of the Torah. And likewise, our sages of blessed memory said "there is no honor but Torah as is stated (Proverbs 3:35) 'The sages shall inherit honor'" (Pirkei Avot 6:3).

Anything other than this is nothing but imaginary and false honor, worthlessness in which there is nothing of avail [Yirmiyahu 16:19]. It is proper for he who aspires to Cleanliness to cleanse and purify himself of this completely. Then he will be successful.

Behold, up till now I have encompassed many details of the particulars of Cleanliness. What has been stated should serve as an example to all of the other Mitzvot and Traits, "let the wise man hear and increase in learning, and the one who understands obtain counsel" (Mishlei 1:5).

I cannot deny that reaching Cleanliness requires a little exertion. Even so, I will say that it does not need as much exertion as it appears. It is more difficult in the thought than in the doing. If a person puts to heart, and fixes constantly in his will to become among those who possess this good trait, behold with a little habituating himself in this, it will come much easier than he could ever imagine. This is something experience can testify to its truth.

Messilat Yesharim

Chapter 12

The true means of acquiring Cleanliness is diligence in study of the words of our sages, of blessed memory, both in matters of Halacha (Jewish law) and in matters of mussar (ethics).

For after a person has truly understood the obligation of Cleanliness and its necessity, having already attained Watchfulness and Zeal by engaging in the means they are acquired and distancing from their detriments, behold, he will no longer have any more obstructions preventing him from attaining Cleanliness except knowledge of the fine details of the Mitzvot in order to guard himself in all of them.

Therefore, he necessarily must attain comprehensive knowledge of the Halachot to their full depth in order to know the extent of reach of the branches of the mitzvot.

Also, since one is prone to forgetfulness in these fine details, he will need diligent study in the books explaining these fine details to renew remembrance of them in his mind. Then certainly, he will be roused to fulfill them.

Likewise, regarding the character traits, it is necessary for him to read the teachings of mussar, whether of the early or later sages. For very often, even after one has resolved to become among the meticulously Clean, he may possibly sin in details he never attained knowledge in.

For man is not born wise and cannot know everything. But by studying the matters, he will be awakened to what he did not know, and he will contemplate on what he did not grasp previously, even matters not found in the books themselves. For when his mind is awakened to the matter, it goes and observes it from all perspectives, and draws forth new understandings from the wellspring of truth.

However, the factors which cause loss of this trait are all those detriments to the trait of Watchfulness, in addition to lack of proficiency in knowledge of the laws and ethics (Mussarim) as I wrote above. Our sages already stated: "an ignorant man cannot be pious" (Avot 2:5). For one who does not know cannot possibly do. Likewise they taught "great is study in that it brings one to doing" (Kidushin 40b).

Messilat Yesharim

Chapter 13

Separation is the beginning of Piety. All that we have explained up to now concerned the requirements needed for a man to become a Tzadik (righteous person). From here on we will discuss the requirements in order to become a Chasid (pious person).

We find that Separation is to Piety as Watchfulness is to Zeal. For the former concerns "turning from evil" (Tehilim 34:14), while the latter concerns "doing good" (ibid).

The general principle of Separation is what our sages of blessed memory said: "sanctify yourself [by abstaining] of what is permitted to you" (Yevamot 20a). This is the meaning of the word "Separation" itself. That is to say - to separate and distance from the thing, prohibiting on oneself something which is permitted. The intent in this is to not come to violate the prohibition itself.

The intent is that a person distance and separate from anything which may lead to something which could bring about evil, even though right now it does not cause evil and even though it is not itself evil.

If you contemplate and consider the matter, you will see that there are three different levels here:

(A) The prohibited things themselves.

(B) Their "fences", namely, the decrees and safeguards instituted by our sages, of blessed memory, enacted for every Jew.

(C) The distancing measures incumbent on every Parush (man of Separation) to make for himself to withdraw in and build [additional] personal fences, namely, to abstain from permitted things themselves which are not forbidden to every Jew and separate from them in order to keep far away from the evil a great distance.

If you ask: On what grounds should we add on additional prohibitions? Our sages of blessed memory already said: "is what the Torah prohibited not enough for you that you seek to forbid on yourself additional matters?!" (Yerushalmi Nedarim 9:1). Surely that which our sages, in their great wisdom, saw necessary to prohibit and make fences they already did so. Thus, that which they left as permitted is because they deemed proper for it to be permitted and not forbidden.

Why then should we now adopt new decrees which they did not see fit to enact? Furthermore, there is no end to this matter. Thus, a man would soon be desolate and afflicted, deriving no enjoyment whatsoever from this world, while our sages, of blessed memory, said: "a person will in the future be held accountable before G-d on all that his eyes beheld and he did not want to eat from it" (Yerushalmi Kidushin 4:12). This is even though it was permitted to him and he had the ability to do so. They brought support for this from scripture: "all that my eyes desired I did not deprive them" (Kohelet 2:10).

The answer to this is that Separation is certainly needed and essential. Our sages of blessed memory exhorted us on this saying (Torat Kohanim 19:2): "'you shall be holy' (Vayikra 19:2) - you shall be Perushim (men of Separation)".

They further said: "whoever fasts is termed 'holy', we can make this inference from the case of a Nazir" (Taanit 11a).

They further said (Pesikta D'Rav Kahana 6:2): "'the righteous man eats to sate his soul' - this refers to Chizkiyahu, King of Judah, whose meal consisted of two bunches of vegetables and a litra of meat. The Jews would mock him saying: 'this is a king?'".

They further said regarding the holy Rabeinu HaKadosh, who before his death lifted his ten fingers and said: "it is revealed and known to You that I did not derive pleasure from this world, not even to my little finger."

They further said (Yalkut Shimoni 247:830): "before a man prays that the words of Torah enter his innards, he should first pray that food and drink not enter them".

All these statements clearly teach the need for Separation and its duty. However, in any case, we must reconcile the statements which indicate the contrary of this.

The explanation is that the matter certainly involves many fundamental distinctions. There is [good] Separation which we are commanded in and there is [bad] Separation which we are warned not to stumble in. This is what king Shlomo said: "do not be overly righteous" (Kohelet 7:16).

We will now explain the good type of Separation. After it has become clear to us that all matters of this world are trials to a man, as we wrote earlier and demonstrated with proofs, and likewise after we have truly realized man's great frailness and his close disposition to all evil, it will perforce be clear that man should do whatever he can to spare himself from these matters in order to protect himself from the evil which is at their feet. For there is no worldly pleasure which does not draw after it some sin in its heel.

For example: food and drink, when clean of all dietary prohibition are permitted to eat. But filling one's belly draws after it removal of the yoke of Heaven, and drinking of wine draws after it licentiousness and other evils. All the more so, once a person habituates himself to satiate [his belly] with food and drink. For then if but one time he lacks fulfilling his habit, it will greatly pain and disturb him.

Due to this, he inserts himself in the rush of business toil and acquiring possessions in order that his table be set as he wishes. From there he is further drawn to wrongdoing and theft, and from there to taking [false] oaths and all other sins which follow. He thus goes away from the divine service, and from Torah study and prayer.

But if from the beginning he had not allowed himself to be drawn after these pleasures, he would have spared himself from all this.

In this way our sages said regarding the rebellious son: "the Torah foresaw his final outcome..." (Sanhedrin 72a).

Similarly, regarding licentiousness they said: "whoever sees the Sotah in her disgrace should make a Nazirite vow against wine"(Sotah 2a).

Observe that this is a great strategy for a man to save himself from his Evil Inclination. Because when a man is engaged in a sin it is very difficult for him to defeat and subdue it. Therefore, it is necessary that while a man is still far from the sin, he keeps his distance. For then it will be difficult for the evil inclination to draw him close to the sin.

Marital relations are completely permitted but the sages decreed immersion in a Mikveh for those who had seminal emissions in order that Torah scholars not be frequently with their wives like roosters. For even though the conjugal act itself is permitted nevertheless he imprints this lust within his nature, and from there he can be drawn to the forbidden as our sages said: "there is a small organ in man. If one satiates it, it becomes hungry. But if he starves it, it becomes satiated" (Sanhedrin 107a).

Not only that but even at the fitting hour and proper time they said of Rabbi Eliezer: "he uncovers a handbreadth and conceals two, and acted as though he were compelled by a demon" (Nedarim 20b), in order to not derive pleasure then.

Regarding clothing and ornaments, the Torah did not issue warnings regarding their beauty or style but rather only that they not contain a mixture of wool and linen and that they be fitted with Tzitzit. Otherwise, they are all permitted.

But who does not know that fancy clothing and ornaments will draw a person to arrogance, and also licentiousness will mix its way in, aside from giving rise to jealousy, lust, and oppressing others which are generated by whatever man deems precious to attain. Our sages already said: "as soon as the Evil Inclination sees a man swinging his heels [when walking], smoothing his garments, and curling his hair, he says - this one is mine!"(Bereishis Raba 22:6).

Strolls and conversations which are not of something prohibited are certainly permitted according to the Torah. But how much neglect of Torah study (bitul Torah) is drawn after this, how much slander, how many lies, how much frivolity. And scripture says: "In the multitude of words, sin is not lacking [but he who holds back his lips is wise]" (Mishlei 10:19).

The general principle: since all matters of this world are nothing but grave dangers, how could he who wants to escape from them and strive to distance from them not be deemed praiseworthy?

This is the good type of Separation, namely, where one takes from the world, in all the uses he makes of it, only that which he is forced to due to the needs of his nature.

This is what Rebbi Yehuda praised himself in the statement I quoted, that he did not derive pleasure from this world, not even for his little finger, although he was Prince of Israel and his table was necessarily a table of kings due to the dignity of his position, as our sages of blessed memory taught: "'two nations are in your womb' (Bereishis 25:23) - this refers to Rebbi and Antoninus, from whose table neither lettuce, nor radish nor cucumber was ever absent either in summer or winter" (Avodah Zarah 11a). This was likewise the case for Chizkiyahu, King of Yehuda.

The other teachings I quoted all support and teach that it is incumbent on a man to separate from all that is [for the sake of] worldly pleasure in order to not fall into its danger.

If you ask: if this is so necessary and essential, why did the sages not decree this like they decreed on the various fences and enactments? The answer is clear and simple for "our sages do not impose an enactment upon the people unless the majority of the public will be able to abide by it" (Bava Kama 79b). The majority of the public are not capable of being Pious so it is sufficient for them that they be Tzadikim (righteous).

But upon the remnant few among the nation who desire to attain closeness to Him, blessed be He, and to benefit, through their attainment, the rest of the masses who depend on them - on them is incumbent to fulfill the Mishna (code) of the Pious which others are not capable of fulfilling.

These duties are the aforementioned orders of Separation. In this G-d has chosen. For it is impossible for the nation that each individual be equal in level because there are various ranks, each man according to his level of understanding.

Behold, at least there should be a few treasured individuals who prepared themselves completely, and through these few the non-prepared will also merit to receive His love, blessed be He, and the indwelling of His Shechina (Divine presence).

As our sages, of blessed memory, expounded on the four species of the Lulav: "let these come and atone on those" (Vayikra Raba 30).

And we find regarding Eliyahu, who answered Rabbi Yehoshua ben Levi in the story of Ula the son of Koshev when the latter said: "is it not a Mishna?" And Eliyahu rebuked him: "But is it a Mishna for the Pious?" (Yerushalmi Terumot 8:10).

But the bad sort of Separation is that of the foolish gentiles who abstain not only from taking of the world the non-essential but also from taking that which is essential. They smite their bodies with sufferings and strange afflictions which G-d does not desire at all. On the contrary, our sages said: "it is forbidden for a man to afflict himself" (Taanit 22b). And regarding charity they said: "whoever needs to take but does not take is as one who sheds blood" (Yerushalmi end of Peah). And likewise, they interpreted: "'a living soul' - the soul that I gave you, keep it alive" (Taanit 22b). And "whoever sits in fast is called a sinner" (Taanit 11b), which they qualified as being in the case where a person is unable to withstand it.

And Hillel would apply the verse: "'the pious man does good to his own soul' (Mishlei 11) to eating the morning meal. He would also wash his face and hands in honor of his Maker, inferring from the practice of washing the statues of kings" (Vayikra Rabba 34).

Here then is a true general principle: whatever worldly matter is not essential for a man, it is proper for him to separate from it, and whatever is essential to him for whatever reason, if he separates from it - he is a sinner, since that thing is necessary for him.

Behold, this is a faithful guideline. But the weighing of this rule is a matter of individual judgment and "according to his understanding a man is praised" (Mishlei 12:8). For it is impossible to discuss all the details of Separation for they are so numerous that a man's mind cannot grasp all of them. Rather each matter must be dealt with in its time.

Messilat Yesharim

Chapter 14

There are three principal divisions of Separation: There is Separation related to the pleasures, Separation related to the laws, and Separation related to the conducts.

Separation related to the pleasures is what we discussed in the previous chapter. Namely, to not take from the world except what necessity forces. This encompasses all that is pleasurable to any one of the senses, whether it be through food, conjugal relations, clothing, strolling, listenings, or in all other similar matters - to partake of them only at days where their enjoyment is a mitzva.

Separation in the laws is to always be stringent in them. To be concerned even for the view of the solitary opinion if its reason has grounds, despite that the Halacha does not follow this opinion. The condition, however, is that his stringency not become a leniency.

Likewise, to be stringent in cases of doubt even in situations where one may be lenient. Our sages, of blessed memory, explained the statement of Yechezkel (Chulin 37b) "'behold my soul never became Tamei (spiritually unclean)' (Yechezkel 4:14) - for I never ate the flesh of an animal which a Sage was called to rule on nor did I ever eat the flesh of an animal about which one says "slaughter it, slaughter it [urgently]". Behold, all these things are certainly permitted according to the Halacha but he was stringent on himself and abstained.

I already explained earlier that what is permitted to the common masses cannot be applied to the Perushim (those who practice Separation) for it is incumbent on them to distance from what is repulsive, or the like and the like of the like. As, Mar Ukba said: "In this matter I am as vinegar derived from wine compared with my father. For if my father were to eat flesh now he would not eat cheese until this very hour tomorrow, whereas I do not eat [cheese] in the same meal but I do eat it in my next meal." (Chulin 105a). There is no question, the Halacha was not like his father did, for if it were, Mar Ukba would not have acted against this. Rather, his father was stringent in this due to his Separation. Therefore, Mar Ukba would call himself "vinegar derived from wine", for he did not measure up in Separation as much as his father.

Separation in conducts consists of secluding and separating oneself from societal company in order to turn one's heart to the divine service and to proper reflection in it. This is on condition that one does not turn in this to the opposite extreme. For our sages, of blessed memory, already said: "a person's mind should always associate with others" (Ketuvot 17a). Likewise they said: "[what is the meaning of the verse] "A sword is upon the boasters (baddim) and they shall become foolish" (Yirmiyahu 50:36) - A sword is upon the enemies of the disciples of the wise, who sit separately [bad bebad] and study Torah. [What is more, they become stupid]" (Makot 10a). Rather, one should associate with the good for whatever time he needs, for his Torah study or livelihood, and then seclude himself afterwards to cling to his G-d, and to attain the ways of the just and the true service.

Included in this [type of separation] is to minimize one's conversation and to guard from idle talk, and not gaze outside one's four cubits, and the like, of the [noble] things a man can habituate himself in until they become as second nature within him.

Even though I have told over to you these three divisions as short general principles, you can nevertheless observe that they encompass many activities of human beings. And I already mentioned to you [last chapter] that it is impossible to set forth the details of their application because personal judgment is required to apply them properly according to the justness and truth of the general principles.

Chapter 15

The best way to acquire Separation is for a man to reflect on the lowliness of the pleasures of this world, their intrinsic baseness, and the great evils that are near to result from them.

For that which inclines one's nature towards these pleasures to the extent that one needs such great strength and so many strategies to separate from them is the enticement of the eyes which tend to be seduced by the superficial appearance of things which appear good and pleasing. This seduction is what brought about the first sin as scripture testifies: "The woman saw that the tree was good to eat, and that it was desirous to the eyes... and she took of its fruit, and ate" (Bereishis 3:6).

But when it becomes clear to a person that this good is completely false, imaginary and ephemeral, while its evil is truly real or truly near to result from, certainly he will become repulsed by it and not desire it in the least. Therefore, this is all of what a person needs to teach his intellect - to recognize the weakness (insignificance) of these pleasures and their falsehood, until on his own, he will be disgusted by them and have no difficulty casting them away.

The pleasure in [eating] food is the most tangible and most felt. Yet, is there anything more swiftly gone and passing than this? For its duration is as the measure of passing a person's throat. After the food passes this point and descends to the intestines, all remembrance of it disappears and is forgotten as if it had never existed. Thus he will be just as satiated if he ate fattened swans than if he had eatened coarse bread in sufficient quantity. All the more so, if he considers the many illnesses brought on through eating, and at least, the heaviness which one feels after a meal and the vapors which darken his intellect. When reflecting on all these things, certainly a person will not desire in this pleasure, since its good is not truly good while its evil is truly evil.

Likewise, for the other pleasures of this world. If he were to reflect on them, he would see that even the imaginary good in them lasts only a brief time, while the evil that may grow out of them is severe and protracted such that no intelligent person would consent to expose himself to these evil dangers for the sake of their small good. This is evident.

When one habituates himself and continuously reflects on this truth, slowly, slowly, he will free himself from this prison of foolishness which the darkness of the physical has shackled him with, and he will no longer be deceived in the least by the enticements of the false pleasures. Then, he will come to be disgusted by them and will realize that he must not take from the world anything but the essential, as I explained earlier.

But just as reflection in this matter causes one to acquire the trait of Separation, so too does ignoring it cause its detriment. Frequenting the aristocrats and the affluent who run after honor and increase vanities. For when one sees their honor and grandeur, it is impossible for lust to not be roused within him to covet them. And even if he does not allow his Evil Inclination to defeat him, nevertheless he will not escape a battle and will thus be in danger. This is as Shlomo said: "It is better to go to a house of mourning than to go to a house of feasting" (Kohelet 7:2).

More important than everything else is solitude. For when he removes worldly matters from before his eyes, so too he removes lust for them from his heart. King David, peace be unto him, praised solitude saying: "Oh, that I had wings like a dove! I would fly away and be at rest; yes, I would wander far away; I would lodge in the wilderness forever" (Tehilim 55:7-8). And we find that the prophets Eliyahu and Elisha would set their dwelling place in the mountains due to their practice of solitude. And the early pious sages, of blessed memory, followed in their footsteps. For they found solitude to be the best path to acquire perfection in Separation, so that the vanities of their neighbors would not lead them to also become vain like them.

That which a person must be cautious of in acquiring Separation is to not desire to skip and jump to the other extreme all at once. For this will certainly not succeed. Rather, he should move gradually in Separation, little by little, acquiring a bit today, and adding a bit more tomorrow, until he habituates so completely that it becomes like second nature to him.

Messilat Yesharim

Chapter 16

Purity is the rectification of the heart and the thoughts. We find this term used by king David who said: "Create in me a pure heart, O G-d" (Tehilim 51:12).

Its matter is for a man to not leave any room in one's deeds for the evil inclination, but rather, that all of his deeds be from the side of wisdom and fear of G-d, and not from the side of sin and lust.

This applies even to bodily and material deeds. For even after a person has accustomed himself in Separation, namely, to not take from the world anything besides the essential, he must still purify his heart and thought, so that even in the little that he takes, he does not have any intent whatsoever to pleasure and lust, but rather to the good that results from deeds, with respect to wisdom and divine service.

This is as they said regarding Rabbi Eliezer: "he would expose one handbreadth and conceal two, and was as one compelled by a demon" (Nedarim 20b). He would not derive any enjoyment whatsoever, and would perform the act only with intent to the mitzva and divine service.

Shlomo said on this: "Know Him in all your ways, and He will straighten your paths" (Mishlei 3:6).

However, you must know that just like Purity of thought applies to the bodily deeds which are intrinsically near to the evil inclination, whereby Purity involves distancing the bodily deeds from the evil inclination such that they don't stem from it, so too Purity of thought applies to the good deeds which are near to the Creator, blessed be He, whereby, Purity involves not distancing from G-d and not stemming from the evil inclination. This is the matter of "not for the sake of the mitzva itself" (Shelo Lishma), mentioned frequently in the words of our sages, of blessed memory.

However, our sages, of blessed memory, have already clarified that there are various levels of "not for the sake of the mitzva itself" (Shelo Lishma).

The worst of all of them is for one to not be serving at all for the sake of divine service, but rather in order to deceive others and to gain money or honor. On this type of person, it was said: "it would have been better had his placenta turned over his face (died in the womb)" (Yerushalmi Berachot 1:5). On such a person, the prophet said: "we are all as one unclean, and all our righteous deeds as like a discarded garment" (Yeshaya 64:5).

There is another type of "not for the sake of the mitzva itself" (Shelo Lishma), which is the "for the sake of receiving a reward" (Avot 1:3). On this our sages said: "a man should always occupy himself with Torah and good deeds, even if it is not for their own sake, for doing so will lead to doing them for their own sake" (Pesachim 50b). Nevertheless, he who has not yet reached from "not for their own sake" (shelo lishma) to "for their own sake" (lishma), is still far from reaching his Shelemut (wholeness/perfection).

However, that which requires deeper analysis and greater work is in mixtures of the forbidden, namely, sometimes a person does a mitzva really for its own sake, namely, that thus our Father decreed, but he cannot refrain from including with it some other motive, such as that other people praise him or that he receive a reward for it. Sometimes, although he does not actually intend that others praise him, nevertheless in rejoicing on the praise received, he puts more effort to improve it. This is similar to the story of Rabbi Chanina ben Teradyon's daughter who was once walking in a graceful manner. When she heard (the Romans) saying: "how beautiful that girl walks", she immediately tried to become more meticulous [in her gracefulness] (Avodah Zara 18a). Hence, this addition stemmed from the spurring of the praise with which they praised her.

Although such a prohibited motive may be annulled in its minor amount [by the major intention], nevertheless a deed with such a mixture is not completely pure. And just like one cannot offer up a flour offering on the altar in the earthly temple unless it is clean, sifted through thirteen sieves (Menachot 76b), so that it is entirely pure of all impurities, so too is it impossible to offer favorably on the heavenly altar, the whole and chosen service of G-d, unless it is the choicest of deeds, entirely pure from all types of impurities.

I am not saying that anything which is not this is completely rejected, for "the Holy One blessed be He does not withhold the reward of any creature" (Pesachim 118b), but He rewards deeds according to what they are. I am referring to the perfect divine service (avodah temima), which is fitting to all those who truly love G-d. It is not proper to call it with this name (avodah temima) except the completely pure service, whose only motive is to G-d, blessed be He, and not to anything else. According to the extent that one is distant from this level, so too will be the extent of his deficiency in it.

This is what king David, peace be unto him, said: "Whom have I in Heaven [but you]? And having You I desire none on earth" (Tehilim 73:25), and likewise "your Word is very pure. therefore, your servant loves it" (Tehilim 119:140). For in truth, the true divine service must be purified far more than gold and silver. This is what was said regarding the Torah: "the Words of G-d are pure words, like silver refined in a furnace on the earth, purified seven times" (Tehilim 12:7).

He who is truly a servant of G-d, will not be satisfied with serving Him minimally. He will not be content to take silver mixed with dross and lead, that is, divine service mixed with impure motivations, but rather only with the clean and pure as is befitting. Then he will be called "one who does a mitzva as it is stated", of which our sages of blessed memory said: "whoever does a mitzva as it is stated, will receive no evil tidings" (Shab.63a). Likewise, they said: "do [good] deeds for the sake of their Maker, and speak of them for their own sake" (Nedarim 62a).

This is what is chosen by those who serve G-d with a whole heart. For he who does not cleave to G-d with a true love will find the purification of this service to be very tedious and burdensome. He will say: "who can possibly withstand this? We are physical creatures, born of woman. It is impossible to attain such great refinement and purification".

But those who love G-d, who desire in His service, will rejoice in demonstrating their faithfulness of love before Him, blessed be He, and in strengthening themselves in refining and purifying it. This is what David himself concluded saying "[Your Word is very pure;] therefore Your servant loves it" (Tehilim 119:140).

In truth, this is the criteria through which the servants of G-d themselves are tested and differentiated in their respective levels. For he who knows more how to purify his heart is likewise drawn closer and is more beloved by

Him, blessed be He. These are the ancient ones in the land, who overcame and were victorious in this area, namely, the forefathers and the other shepherds who purified their hearts before Him. This is what David exhorted his son Shlomo: "[know the G-d of your father and serve Him with a perfect heart and with a willing mind]. For the L-rd searches all hearts and understands all the imaginations of the thoughts"(Divrei Hayamim 28:9).

And as our sages, of blessed memory, said: "G-d wants the heart"(Sanhedrin 106b).

For to the Master of the world, the deeds alone are not sufficient, namely, to perform an act of mitzva. Rather, the primary importance before Him is that the heart be pure, so that its intent is to true service.

The heart is the king and mover of all other parts of the body and the leader over all of them. If the heart does not bring itself to serve Him, blessed be He, the service of the other limbs are worth nothing. For wherever the spirit of the heart goes, they will follow along as scripture states explicitly: "Give your heart to Me my son"(Mishlei 23:26).

Messilat Yesharim

Chapter 17

The way to attain this trait is easy for one who has already strove and attained all the aforementioned traits. For when one thinks and contemplates on the lowliness of the pleasures of this world and its good, as I wrote earlier, he will come to despise them, and will not consider them to be anything but evils and lackings of the dark and coarse physical nature. When the truth ingrains within him of their being real lackings and evils, certainly it will become easier for him to separate from them and remove them from his heart.

Therefore, the deeper and more diligently he delves in his thoughts into recognizing the lowliness of the physical and its pleasures, the easier it will be for him to purify his thoughts and heart so that he does not turn at all to the evil inclination in anything whatsoever. Rather, his physical deeds will be as one forced and not otherwise.

However, just like we have divided purity of thought into two divisions, namely, the bodily actions and the actions of Divine service, so too the in-depth contemplation necessary to acquire purity in them divides into two divisions.

To purify the thoughts in the bodily actions, one needs to diligently observe the lowliness of this world and its pleasures, as I wrote. While to purify the actions of Divine service, one needs to contemplate much on the deceit of honor and its falsehood, and to habituate oneself to flee from it.

Then, one will be clean from striving for the praise and lauding of other people when serving G-d. His thought will turn solely to our Master (G-d), who is our praise, and who is all our good and perfection, and beside Whom there is nothing else, as it is written: "He is your praise and He is your G-d" (Devarim 10:21).

One of the means which lead a person to acquire this trait is to prepare oneself for Divine service and mitzvot, namely, to not enter suddenly in performing a mitzva. For then, one's mind is not yet composed and is unable to think on what he is doing. Rather, one should ready himself to the matter and slowly prepare his heart for reflection.

Then let him contemplate what he is going to do and before Whom he is going to do it. For when he enters in this contemplation, it will be easy for him to cast away external motives, and to implant in his heart the true and desirable motive.

Note that the early pious men of old would wait one hour before prayer, in order to direct their hearts to G-d (Berachot 30b). There is no doubt that they wouldn't waste an hour of time. Rather they would direct and prepare their hearts for the prayer they needed to pray, pushing out foreign thoughts and filling themselves with the requisite fear and love of G-d. On this it is written: "If you prepared your heart, then spread out your hands to Him" (Iyov 11:13).

The detriments of this trait are lack of reflecting on the aforementioned matters, namely, ignorance of the lowliness of the worldly pleasures, pursuit of honor, and insufficient preparation before G-d's service.

The former two entice the mind and draw it towards ulterior motives, like an adulterous wife who, while still married to her husband, takes other men. Ulterior thoughts are referred to as "lewdness of the heart", as written: "and you shall not stray after your hearts and after your eyes which you go after promiscuously (Zonim)" (Bamidbar 15:39). For the heart strays from the whole aspiration which it should have bonded to, and turns instead to the worthless and imaginary falsehood.

Insufficient preparation for Divine service causes the natural foolishness which comes from the side of physicality to not be divested from within oneself. Thus he rottens the Divine service with its stench.

We will now explain the trait of Piety.

Messilat Yesharim

Chapter 18

The trait of piety truly requires a great explanation. For there are many practices and ways which circulate among many people as piety but which are nothing but the shells of piety, lacking in shape, form and correction.

This stems from a lack of true in-depth study and thought on the part of these practitioners [of the shells of piety]. For they did not toil and strain themselves to attain a clear and correct knowledge of the way of G-d. But instead, they went and adopted whatever practices struck them as being pious according to first thought, without delving deeply into the matters and weighing them on the scales of wisdom.

These people have given Piety a repulsive odor in the eyes of most people, including the intelligent among them, leading them to think Piety consists of foolish things and is counter to intelligence and sound knowledge. The masses came to believe Piety consists of nothing but reciting numerous supplications and lengthy confessions, great wailings and prostrations, strange afflictions through which a man kills himself such as immersing in ice [water] and snow, and the like

They do not realize that even while a bit of these things may be needed for sinners engaged in repentance and some for those who practice Separation (Perushim), but piety is not founded on these matters at all. Only the good of these practices are fit to accompany Piety.

But actual Piety itself requires great depth to understand it correctly. It is based on foundations of great wisdom and utmost rectification of one's deeds, which befits every wise hearted man to pursue. For only the wise can truly attain it, as our sages stated: "an unlearned man cannot be pious" (Avot 2:5).

We will now explain this matter in proper order.

The root of piety is what our sages, of blessed memory, stated: "Fortunate is the man whose toil is in the Torah and gives gratification to his Maker" (Berachot 17a).

The [explanation of the] matter is as follows. It is known which mitzvot are binding on every Jew and the extent their obligation reaches.

But he who truly loves the Creator, blessed be He, will not strive and intend to discharge himself with the known obligations binding on every Jew. Rather, what will happen to him is the same as that of a son who loves his father. Even if his father reveals a slight indication of something he desires, already the son will strive greatly, to the best of his ability, to fulfill this thing or service. Even though the father merely mentioned it once and only halfway, this will be enough for such a son to understand the direction of his father's intent and to do for him even what he did not say explicitly. For he can deduce on his own that this thing will bring pleasure to his father, and he will not wait until his father commands him more explicitly or tells him another time.

With our own eyes we can observe this matter occurring at all times and in all places between all friends and lovers, between man and wife, between father and son.

The general principle: wherever the love between two is true and strong, one will not say to the other: "No more was requested of me. It's enough for me to do what I was told explicitly". Rather through what one requested, the other will infer the requester's intent and will strive to do what he deems will be pleasing to the other.

Similar to this will occur to he who loves his Creator with a faithful love. For G-d is also a class of those who are loved. Thus, the mitzvot which are clear and familiar will be to him only as a revelation of intent, to indicate to him that the will and desire of G-d inclines in the direction of that principle. Then, he will not say to himself "it is enough for me what was stated explicitly", or "I will discharge my duty with what is nonetheless incumbent upon me". Rather, on the contrary, he will say "since I discovered and saw that G-d's desire inclines to this, this will be a guide for me to increase in this matter and to expand it in all directions which I can infer that His will desires. Such a person is called: "one who gives gratification to his Maker".

Hence, the general matter of Piety is to expand the fulfillment of all the mitzvot in all sides and conditions which are proper and possible.

You can see that Piety is related to Separation. Only that Separation is in the negative commandments while Piety is in the positive commandments. But both are of the same matter, namely, to add on to what was explicitly stated in the mitzvot what we can deem will be pleasing before G-d, blessed be He. This is the definition of true Piety.

We will now explain its primary divisions.

Messilat Yesharim

Chapter 19

There are three primary divisions of Piety. The first relates to deed, the second to manner of performance, and the third to intent.

The first division of deed itself further divides into two subdivisions. The first between man and G-d and the second between man and his fellow.

The first subdivision of the first division, namely, piety in deed between man and G-d, its matter is for a person to fulfill the mitzvot in all their fine details to the furthest extent of one's ability. Our sages, of blessed memory, called these "the remnants of a mitzva". They said: "the remnants of the mitzvot prevent divine punishment" (Sukkah 38a). For even though the body of a mitzvah is fulfilled without them and one has already discharged his obligation, nevertheless, this is sufficient for the general masses of the Jewish people. But those who are Pious must only increase fulfillment in the mitzvot and not omit any detail whatsoever of them.

CHESED - KINDLINESS: The second subdivision of the first division, namely, piety in deed between man and his fellow, its matter is great beneficence, namely, that one always does good to others and never harms them. This applies to the body, possessions, and spirit of one's fellow.

Body: that one strives to help all men however he can, and lighten the burden that is upon them. As we learned: "bearing the yoke with one's fellow" (Avot 6:6). If his fellow is about to be struck by some bodily harm and he can prevent it or remove it, he should exert himself to do so.

Possessions: to assist him with whatever means he can and to prevent damages from befalling him however he can. It goes without saying that the pious person will distance all possibilities of damages to individuals or the public that may arise from his own part.

And even though there is no immediate likelihood of damage, since it may potentially lead to this, he will remove it and dispose of it. Our sages, of blessed memory, said: "the possessions of your fellow should be as precious to you as your own" (Avot 2:12).

Spirit: to strive to bring however much contentment to his fellow that he can. This applies to matters of honor or any other area. If he knows that he can do something to his fellow that will give him contentment, it is a mitzvah of Piety to do so. It goes without saying that he will not cause him any pain of any kind whatsoever.

The general matter of all this is "acts of kindliness", which our sages, of blessed memory, greatly emphasized to us on its great worth and our obligation in it. Included in this is to "pursue peace", which is the general beneficence between every man and his fellow.

I will now bring you proofs on all this from the words of our sages, of blessed memory, even though these things are evident and do not require the support of proofs.

In the chapter "Bnei HaIr" (Megilah 27b): "Rabbi Zakkai was asked by his disciples: 'in virtue of what have you merited such long life?' He replied: Never in my life have I made water within four cubits of a place where prayer is said, nor have I called my fellow by a nickname, nor have I missed making Kiddush on the [Sabbath] day. I had an old mother who once sold her headdress so as to bring me [wine for] the Kiddush".

We see from here an example of piety with regard to the fine points of the mitzvot. For he was already exempt from acquiring wine for Kiddush since he did not have enough [money] to such an extent that his mother needed to sell her own headdress. For him to do so was thus out of the trait of Piety.

With regard to the honor of his fellow, he would not call his fellow a nickname, even one which is not derogatory as Tosfot explained there.

There, Rav Huna also tied a reed string around his garment because he had sold his waistband to buy wine for Kiddush.

Also there, "Rabbi Eliezer ben Shammua was asked by his disciples: "In virtue of what have you merited such a long life? He replied: Never in my life have I made a shortcut through a synagogue, nor have I walked over the heads of the holy people (his students)."

Behold this trait is regarding showing respect to the synagogue and showing respect to other people, to not step over their sitting place so as not to appear to be degrading them.

Also there: "Rabbi Peridah was asked by his disciples: In virtue of what have you merited such a long life? He replied: Never in my life did anyone arrive before me at the house of study, nor have I said the blessing before a Kohen, nor have I ever eaten meat of an animal from which the priestly portions had not been taken.

Also there: "Rabbi Nehunia was asked by his disciples: In virtue of what have you merited such a long life? He replied: Never in my life have I sought honor through the degradation of my fellow, nor has the curse of my fellow gone up with me upon my bed".

This was explained there by illustration: "Rav Huna was once carrying a spade on his shoulder. When Rav Hana bar Hanilai wanted to take it from him, Rav Huna said to him: 'if you are accustomed to carry in your own town, take it, but if not, I do not wish to be paid honor through your degradation'".

Hence, even though the implication of "honoring oneself through the degradation of one's fellow" is that one tries to put down his fellow in order to increase one's own honor. But the pious will not consent to degrade him even if the fellow himself comes and willingly desires this.

Similar to this Rabbi Zeira said: "Never in my life have I been impatient with my household, nor have I walked ahead of one greater than myself, nor have I meditated on the Torah in filthy alleys, nor have I walked four cubits without Torah or Tefilin, nor have I slept in the Beit Hamidrash (house of Torah study), either a long or a short nap, nor have I rejoiced in the downfall of my fellow, nor have I called another person by his nickname" (ibid).

Here we have examples of acts of piety in all the ways we mentioned above.

Our sages, of blessed memory, further said (Bava Kama 30a): "Rabbi Yehuda said: 'he who wishes to become pious, let him fulfill the matters of Berachot (blessings)' (this is for those things between man and his Maker), some say 'let him fulfill the laws of damages' (this is for those things between man and his fellow), and some say 'let him fulfill the matters of Pirkei Avot' (which include matters from all the divisions of piety).

Behold acts of kindliness are of great primary importance to the Chasid (pious). For the term "Chasidut" itself comes from the term "kindliness" (Chesed). And our sages, of blessed memory, said (Pirkei Avot 1:2): "on three things the world stands", and one of whom is "acts of kindliness". Likewise, they counted them as one of those things which a person "eats of its fruits in this world while the principal [reward] is reserved for him in the World to Come."

Our sages further taught: "Rabbi Simlai expounded: 'the Torah begins and ends with acts of kindnesses'" (Sotah 14a).

Rava expounded: "whoever has these three traits is surely of the seed of Avraham our forefather: mercy, shame, and benevolence" (Yevamot 79a).

Rabbi Eleazar stated, acts of kindness are greater than charity, for it is said (Hoshea 10:12): "sow to yourselves according to your charity, but reap according to your kindness (Chesed)" (Sukkah 49b).

Our Rabbis taught: "in three respects are acts of kindness (Gemilut Chasadim) superior to charity: charity can be done only with one's money, but acts of kindness can be done with one's person and one's money. Charity can be given only to the poor, acts of kindness are both to the rich and the poor. Charity can be given to the living only, acts of kindness can be done both to the living and to the dead alike" (Sukkah 49b).

They further said: "'And he shall give you mercy, and have mercy upon you' (Devarim 13:17) - anyone who is merciful to others, will be shown mercy by Heaven" (Shabbat 151b).

This is obvious, for the Holy One, blessed be He, repays measure for measure (Sanhedrin 90a). Thus, he who has mercy and does kindness with others, will also be shown mercy when he is judged and pardoned of his sins with kindliness. For such pardoning is justice, since it corresponds measure for measure to his practice. This is what our sages, of blessed memory, taught: "who is forgiven iniquity? he who overlooks transgression [committed against himself]" (Rosh Hashana 17a).

But he who is not willing to overlook transgression [against himself], or act with kindliness, justice dictates that he too will be dealt with only strict justice. Now see - who is there and is there anyone who could stand up if the Holy One, blessed be He, were to hold him up to strict justice?! King David prayed saying: "do not enter into judgment with Your servant, for no living being can be found vindicated before You" (Tehilim 143:2).

But he who does kindness will receive kindness, and the more he does, the more he will receive. David would exult in possessing this good trait, striving to do kindness even to those who hated him, as written "but when they were sick, my clothing was sackcloth; I afflicted my soul with fastings" (Tehilim 35:13), and "if I have repaid the one who did evil to me" (Tehilim 7:5).

Included in this matter is to not cause pain to any creature, even animals, and to show mercy and concern towards them. Likewise, scripture states: "the righteous man knows the soul of his beast" (Mishlei 12:10) (Rashi-what his beast needs), and according to some of our sages (Shabbat 128b), to cause pain to an animal is a biblical prohibition, while to others it is at least a Rabbinical prohibition.

The general principle of the matter is that mercy and benevolence must be permanently fixed in the heart of the Chasid (pious person), and that his aspiration is always be to bring contentment to his fellow creatures and not cause them any pain, etc.

FEAR OF G-D: The second division of piety relates to manner of performance. This too divides into two areas which, however, contain many details. These two primary areas are fear and love - the two pillars of true service of G-d, without which it cannot at all be established.

Included in fear [of G-d] is submission before G-d, to feel shame in approaching His service, honoring His commandments, His blessed Name, and His Torah.

Included in love [of G-d] is joy, clinging, and jealousy. We will know clarify them one by one.

The primary aspect of fear of G-d is fear (awe) of His exaltedness. A person must think when he is engaged in prayer or performing a mitzva, that it is before the King of kings that he is praying or performing the mitzva. This is what the Tanna exhorts us saying: "when you pray, know before Whom you are praying" (Berachot 28b).

In order to reach this fear, a man must reflect on and contemplate well three things: first, that he is actually (mamash) standing before the Creator, blessed be He, engaging in a give and take with Him, even though a man's eye does not see Him. You will observe that this is the most difficult for a person to form a true image in his heart because his senses do not at all aid in this.

However, he who is of sound intellect can establish in his heart the truth of the matter, with a little contemplation and attention, how he comes and quite literally engages in a give and take with G-d, blessed be He, pleading before Him, and beseeching Him, while G-d, blessed be His Name, lends ear to him, gives attention to his words, just like when a man speaks to his neighbor and the neighbor attentively listens to his words.

After one has established this in his knowledge, he must then contemplate on G-d's exaltedness, blessed be He, that He is exalted and elevated over all blessing and praise, over all forms of perfection that our minds can possibly imagine and comprehend.

He must also contemplate on the lowliness of man and his baseness due to his physical nature and grossness, and all the more so due to all the sins he committed in his life.

When he contemplates all of this, it will be impossible for his heart to not fear and for him to not quiver while he speaks his words before Him, blessed be He, and utters His Name, and strives to find His favor. This is what scripture says: "Serve G-d with fear, and rejoice in trembling" (Tehilim 2:11), and "G-d is revered in the great council of the holy ones and feared by all around Him"(Tehilim 89:8).

For the angels are closer to Him due to lacking physical bodies. Thus, it is easier for them to conceive of His exalted greatness. Therefore, His fear weighs upon them more strongly than upon human beings. However, king David would praise G-d saying: "I shall prostrate myself to the Temple of Your holiness in fear of You" (Tehilim 5:8), and scripture says: "and he was afraid before My Name" (Malachi 2:5), and "my G-d, I am ashamed and blush to lift up my face to You" (Ezra 9:6).

However, this fear must first grow strong in one's heart and afterwards its effects will also manifest in the limbs of the body, namely, a bowed head and prostration, lowering of the eyes and clasping of the hands, as a lowly slave before a great king. Likewise, they said in the Gemara "Rava clasped his hands and prayed, saying, 'I am like a slave before his Master'" (Shabbat 10a).

We have spoken till now on submission and shame. We will now speak on the matter of honor.

HONOR: Our sages, of blessed memory, have already exhorted us on the honor and dignity of a mitzva. They expounded (Shabbat 133b): "'this is my G-d, and I will beautify Him' (Shemot 15:2) - beautify yourself before Him in [the fulfillment of] mitzvot. Thus, make beautiful Tzitzit, beautiful Tefilin, a beautiful Sukkah, a beautiful Torah scroll, [and write it with fine ink, a fine reed, and a skilled penman, and wrap it about with beautiful silks]...". They also said: "A person should spend an extra third to beautify a Mitzvah. Up to this extra third, is on him. Above a third, the Holy One, blessed be He, returns the money to him (in this world)" (Bava Kama 9b). Thus, the intent of their words is quite clearly spoken, that the performance of the mitzva by itself is not enough. Rather, one must also honor and beautify it.

This comes to exclude the view of those who, in order to make things easier for themselves, will claim: "honor is only for human beings who are seduced by such vanities. But the Holy One, blessed be He, is not concerned for such things, for He is above these things and elevated above them. As long as the mitzva is done correctly, this is sufficient."

The truth, however, is that the L-rd, blessed be He, is called "the G-d of honor" (Tehilim 29:3), and we are under duty to honor Him, even though He does not need our honor and it is neither important nor significant to Him.

Nevertheless, he who diminishes this honor to G-d when he was able to increase it is considered a sinner. This is what the prophet Malachi rebuked the Jews with the word of G-d saying: "If you offer a blind [animal] for a sacrifice, is it not evil? Were you to offer it to your governor, will he accept it from you or will he show you favor?" (Malachi 1:8).

Our sages, of blessed memory, exhorted us to conduct ourselves in the opposite manner in the divine service. For instance, regarding water which became uncovered, that one must not filter them with a strainer to permit their use [for temple purposes]. They gave the reason: "when was this permitted? [answer:] For mundane use. But was this ever permitted for Temple use!? It is disqualified from the verse 'Were you to offer it to your governor, will he accept it from you or show you favor?'" (Malachi 1:8)".

Observe, what defect is there in strained water which are already permitted for mundane use? But even so, they are forbidden for temple use because it is not honorable.

They further said in Sifri (Devarim Piska 68): "'and all your choice vows' (Devarim 12:11) - one should bring only from the choicest."

We also find by Kayin and Hevel (Bereishis Raba 22:5): "Hevel brought from the first born of his sheep and of their fats". While, as they explained, Kayin brought from among the worst of the fruits of the land. What was the result? "and the L-rd turned to Hevel and his offering, but for Kayin and his offering He paid no heed" (Bereishis 4:5).

It is further written: "But cursed be the deceiver who has in his flock a male, yet he vows and sacrifices to the L-rd a blemished one. For I am a great King [says the L-rd of Hosts]" (Malachi 1:14).

Our sages, of blessed memory, exhorted us in many places against the disrespect of Mitzvot. They said: "whoever holds a Torah scroll which is uncovered, will be buried naked" (Shabbat 14a), because of the disrespect to the mitzva.

The order of offering the first fruits (Bikurim) are a guide for us to see what is "Hidur Mitzva" (beautifying a mitzva). We learned: "an ox with horns overlaid with gold and with an olive crown upon its head walks before them..." (Bikurim 3:3). And later on there: "the wealthy brought their first fruits in baskets of gold, while the poor used baskets of willow branches" (Bikurim 3:8). And "there are three elements in first fruits: the first fruits themselves, the additions to the first fruits, and the decorations of the first fruits..." (Bikurim 3:10). Thus we see just how much it is proper to add on to the body of the mitzva itself in order to beautify it. From here we learn to all the other Mitzvot of the Torah.

They further said (Shabbat 10a): "Rava would don a cloak and pray, saying: 'prepare to meet your G-d, O Israel' (Amos 4:12)".

They further said on the verse: "'then Rivkah took the finest clothes of Eisav her older son' (Gen 27:15) - Raban Shimon ben Gamliel says: 'I served my father... but when Eisav served his father, he would only do so while wearing royal clothing'" (Bereishis Raba 65:16).

Behold, if this is so for flesh and blood, how much more so, for the King of kings, the Holy One, blessed be He, that one who stands before Him to pray should wear honorable clothing, and sit before him as one who sits before a great king.

Included in this category, is honoring the Sabbath and Festivals. For whoever gives much honor to these, certainly brings gratification to his Maker, who thus commanded us: "you shall honor it" (Isaiah 58:13).

Once it has become established to us as truth that honoring the Sabbath is a mitzva, there are many different ways to honor it. But the general principle is that any action which shows importance to the Sabbath, we should do.

Therefore, the early sages occupied themselves in the preparation of the Sabbath, each sage according to his own way: "Rabbi Abahu used to sit on an ivory stool and fan the fire. Rav Safra would roast the head of an animal. Raba salted fish. Rav Huna would light the lamp. Rav Papa plaited the wicks. Rav Chisda cut beets. Rabbah and Rav Joseph chopped wood. Rav Nachman bar Isaac carried things in and out, saying: 'If Rav Ammi and Rav Assi visited me, would I not carry thus for them?'" (Shabbat 119a).

Notice, the comparison of Rav Nachman which contains a model for us to learn from. For he would contemplate what he would do for a person he wishes to honor and then would do a similar thing for the Sabbath.

On this matter it was said: "a person should always be clever in the fear of Heaven" (Berachot 17a) - to know and deduce one thing from another, and to devise new ways of bringing gratification to his Maker in every possible manner.

For when we recognize G-d's great loftiness above us, any connection to Him which He grants us should be deemed by us to be a tremendous honor. Since, He in His great goodness and despite all of our lowliness, chose, in His humility, to bestow honor on us and give us His holy words. We should then, at the very least, honor them with all our strength and demonstrate the extent of their esteem to us.

You will observe that this is the true fear of G-d, Yirat Haromemut (fear of His exaltedness) which we mentioned. Honor out of this type of fear is near to the feelings of intense love which endears [the service of G-d], as I will explain further with G-d's help. This is not so for the "fear of punishment" which is not the primary fear and which does not lead to these good traits.

Let us return to the matter of [honoring] the Sabbath. Our sages said: "Rav Anan wore [black] overalls" (Shabbat 119a), i.e. he would wear a black garment on Friday so that the honor of the Sabbath would be more recognizable when he donned fine [Shabbat] clothing.

Hence, not only the actual preparation for the Sabbath is included in [the mitzvah of] honor, but even its contrast when it serves to augment the honor of Sabbath is also included in the Mitzva. Thus, they prohibited one to fix a meal before the Sabbath due to the honor of the Sabbath (Gitin 38b), and other similar prohibitions.

Further included in fear is honoring the Torah and those who study it. We learned explicitly: "Whoever honors the Torah, is himself honored by the people" (Avot 4:6). And our sages, of blessed memory, said:

Rabbi Yochanan said: Why did Achav merit royalty for twenty-two years? - Because he honored the Torah, which was given in twenty-two letters, as it is written (I Kings 20:9), "And he sent messengers to Achav... it shall be, that whatever is the desire of your eyes, they shall put in their hand, and take it away... And he said to the messengers of Ben-Hadad, tell my lord the king, all that you did send for to your servant at the first I will do; but this thing I may not do." Now what is meant by 'whatever is the desire of your eyes'? Surely the Scroll of the Torah!" (Sanhedrin 102b).

They further said: "if a man was carrying [a sefer Torah] from one place to another, he should not put it in a saddle-bag and place it on his donkey and ride on it. Rather, he should carry the scroll on his lap" (Berachot 18a).

It was also forbidden to sit on a bed which a Torah scroll lies upon (Moed Katan 25a). Likewise, they said: "it is forbidden to throw out holy writings, even Halachot (laws) and Agadot" (Eruvin 98a, Rambam Hilchot Sefer Torah ch.10). Likewise, they forbade putting books of the Prophets and Writings on top of the Five Books of Moses (Megilah 27a). These are things that our sages, of blessed memory, forbade on the entire congregation of Israel. But the Chasid should learn from them and add on them in various ways for the honor of the Name of the L-rd, his G-d.

Included in this category is the cleanliness and purity required for the words of Torah - to not study the Torah, in filthy places, even if this is only in thought, nor with unclean hands. Our sages already abundantly warned us on this in many places (ex.Yoma 30a).

Regarding those who study the Torah, scripture states: "you shall rise before an elder and respect the face of the learned" (Vayikra 19:32). From which we learn all ways of honors that it is possible to confer to Torah scholars, which are certainly proper for the Chasid to do.

Our sages of blessed memory expounded (Ketuvot 103b): "'he honors those who fear G-d' (Tehilim 15:4) - this refers to Yehoshafat King of Judah, who, whenever he saw a Torah scholar, would rise up from his throne, hug him, kiss him, and say to him: 'Rebbi, Rebbi, my teacher, my teacher'".

When Rebbi Zeira was weak from his studies, he would sit at the entrance of the Beit Midrash (house of Torah study), to perform the mitzva of standing up for Torah scholars.

All these are things which the Creator, blessed be He, has shown us that He desires in, and has revealed to us His exalted judgment in this.

Since it is so, one who wishes to bring gratification to his Maker, should walk in this path, and increase strategies for doing what is just before the blessed G-d.

Also included in this area is honoring the synagogue and the house of study (Orach Chaim 151). For not only must one refrain from acting frivolously there, but he should act with all kinds of honor and fear in all of his conducts and actions. Whatever he would not do in the palace of a great king, he should not do in them.

LOVE OF G-D: Let us now speak on the matter of love [of G-d]. Its branches are three: joy, clinging, and jealousy.

The matter of love of G-d is that a person actually yearns and lusts for closeness to G-d, blessed be He, and chases His holiness as one chases something he desires intensely. This is to the extent that merely mentioning His Name, speaking of His praises, and occupying himself with the words of His Torah or divinity literally becomes a delight and pleasure, as one who strongly loves the wife of his youth or his only son, so that even speaking of them gives him gratification and pleasure. This is as scripture states: "[Is Ephraim my dear son? Is he my delightful child?] For whenever I speak of him, I will remember him still"(Yirmiyahu 31:19).

Certainly, one who loves his Creator a true love, will not forgo His service for any reason in the world, unless he is actually forced.

He will not need any persuasion nor enticement to serve Him. Rather, on the contrary, his heart will lift him and rush him to it, unless there is some great barrier that blocks him.

Behold, this is the precious trait which the Pious men of old, the lofty holy ones had merited to attain. As king David said: "As a hart cries longingly for the water brooks, so does my soul cry longingly to You, O G-d; My soul thirsts for G-d, for the living G-d; when shall I come and appear before G-d?" (Tehilim 42:2-3), and "My soul yearns, yes, faints for the courts of the L-rd" (Tehilim 84:3), "My soul thirsts for You; my flesh longs for You..." (Tehilim 63:2). All this due to his powerful yearning to the blessed G-d.

This is likewise as the prophet said: "to Your Name and to Your remembrance is the lust of [our] soul" (Isaiah 26:8), and "my soul yearns for You in the night; my spirit within me seeks You" (Isaiah 26:9). And David himself said: "when I remember You on my bed, through the night watches I meditate about You" (Tehilim 63:7). Thus, he described the pleasure and delight he experienced when speaking of and praising G-d, blessed be His Name. Likewise, he said: "I will delight myself in Your Commandments, which I love" (Tehilim 119:47), and "Your testimonies are my delight..." (Tehilim 119:24).

This love certainly must not be a "love which depends on something" (Avot 5:16). Namely, that one should love the blessed Creator, not because He bestows good to him and grants him wealth and success. Rather, it should be like the love of a son for his father, which is actually (mamash) a natural love, to which the son's nature compels and forces him to this. As scripture states: "is He not your Father, your Master?" (Devarim 32:6).

The test of this type of love comes during times of difficulties and troubles. As our sages, of blessed memory, said (Berachot 54a): "'You shall love the L-rd your G-d with all your heart and with all your soul [and with all your might]' (Devarim 6:5): 'with all your soul' - even if He takes your soul. 'with all your might' - with all your possessions."

However, in order that the troubles and distress not become difficulties and impediments to the love of G-d, a person should console himself with two understandings, one is suitable to everyone, and the second is for the wise who possess depth of understanding.

The first understanding: "All that G-d does is for the good" (Berachot 60b). For even this pain and difficulty which appears to one's eyes as evil, is in truth nothing but true good. It is analogous to a doctor which must cut away flesh or amputate an infected limb so that the rest of the body may heal and not die. Even though the act appears at first to be cruel, it is really an act of true mercy, in order to eventually benefit him in the end. The patient will not cease to love the doctor due to this act. Rather, on the contrary, he will love him even more.

So too here, when a person considers that all of what the Holy One, blessed be He, does with him, whether to his body or to his possessions - is for his own good. Even though he does not see nor understand how this is for his good, nevertheless, there is no doubt that it is indeed for his own good. Then, one's love for G-d will not become weakened from all difficulties and sufferings. Rather, on the contrary, it will intensify and increase in him always.

But those of true understanding do not need even this reason. For they are not to be motivated by their own interests at all. Rather, all of their aim is to increase the honor of His Name, blessed be He, and to bring gratification to Him. The more the impediments against them increase, so that they will require more strength to overcome them, the more they will strengthen their hearts and rejoice to demonstrate the strength of their faith. They are as a military general, distinguished for his bravery, who always chooses the most difficult battle, to demonstrate his prowess in emerging victorious.

This matter is familiar by every lover of flesh and blood who will rejoice when given an opportunity to show the subject of his love just how powerful is the extent of his love to his beloved.

Let us now explain the branches of love. They are the three I mentioned earlier: clinging, joy, and jealousy.

CLINGING: The matter of clinging is when a person's heart clings so much to the blessed G-d that he ceases to turn or take interest in anything else but Him. This is what Shlomo brought by way of analogy: "a lovely hind and a graceful doe, her breasts will satisfy you at all times; you shall always be infatuated with her love" (Mishlei 5:19). And in the Talmud, our sages, of blessed memory stated (Eruvin 54b): "It was said of Rebbi Eliezar ben Pedat that he sat and studied Torah in the lower market of Tzipori while his cloak lay in the upper market of the town". The ultimate goal of this trait is for a person to cling thus to His Creator at all times, and at every moment. But at the least, if he loves his Creator, certainly he will cling to Him in this manner during the times of his [divine] service.

In the Talmud Yerushalmi it is reported: "While Rabbi Chanina ben Dosa was standing in prayer a poisonous lizard came and bit him but he did not interrupt his prayer... His disciples asked him: 'Rabeinu! Did you not feel anything?! He replied to them: 'I swear that due to my heart being intent on the prayer, I felt nothing'"

The Torah exhorts us many times on the clinging [to G-d]: "to love the L-rd your G-d. and to cling to Him" (Devarim 30:20), "to Him shall you cling" (Devarim 10:20, 13:5). And David said: "my soul clings to You" (Tehilim 63:9). All these verses speak of one matter, namely, the clinging with which a man clings to G-d, blessed be He, to such an extent that he is unable to part or move from Him.

And our sages of blessed memory said: "Rabbi Shimon ben Lakish said: 'the Holy One, blessed be He, used three expressions of love regarding the Jewish people, and we learn all of them from the account of Shechem ben Chamor: 'clinging', 'yearning', and 'desire'" (Gen. Rabbah 80:7). These are actually (mamash) the three main branches of love, namely, the yearning I mentioned, the clinging, and the pleasure and joy felt by the lover when engaged in matters of his beloved.

JOY: The second [branch of love of G-d] is joy, it is a great, essential principal in serving G-d. This is what David exhorted us saying: "Serve G-d with joy, come before Him with song" (Tehilim 100:2), and "the righteous will rejoice, they will exult before God and delight with joy" (Tehilim 68:4). And our sages said: "the Divine presence rests on a person only through his rejoicing in a mitzva" (Shabbat 30b). On the aforementioned verse: "Serve G-d with joy", our sages said in a Midrash (Shocher Tov, Tehilim 100): "Rabbi Abahu says: 'when you stand to pray, your heart should rejoice, for you are praying to the Almighty of whom there is none like Him'".

For this is the true joy, namely, that a person's heart delight that he merits to serve before the blessed Master, of whom there is none like Him, and to toil in His Torah and His mitzvot which are the true perfection and the eternal worth. And Shlomo said in a parable on wisdom: "Draw me, we will run after You. The King has brought me into His chambers; we will be glad and rejoice in You" (Shir HaShirim 1:4). For the further a person merits to enter into the inner chambers of knowledge of His blessed greatness, the more his joy will increase and his heart will sing within him. And scripture states: "Israel will rejoice in its Maker; the children of Zion will exult in their King" (Tehilim 149:2).

And David when he had already reached this level a great measure said: "May my words be pleasing to Him; I shall rejoice in G-d" (Tehilim 104:34), and "I will come to the altar of God, to God my exceeding joy, and I will thank You with a lyre, O G-d, My G-d" (Tehilim 43:4). And he said: "My lips sing praises, when I sing to You, and my soul which You have redeemed" (Tehilim 71:23).

For the joy had grown so intensely within him when he would engage in the blessed G-d's praises that his lips would already move and sing on their own. All this was due to the great flaming of his soul which was ablaze with joy before G-d. This is what he concludes "and my soul which You have redeemed".

We find that the Holy One, blessed be He, complained to the Jewish people for lacking this condition in their service, as written: "because you did not serve the L-rd, your G-d, with joy and gladness of heart" (Devarim 28:47).

So when David saw the Jews reaching this level when they donated to the construction of the Temple, he prayed that this good trait should remain with them and not leave them as written: "and now I have seen with joy Your people who are present here, offer willingly to You. O L-rd, G-d of Abraham, Isaac, and Israel, our forefathers, preserve this eternally, even the inclination of the thoughts of the heart of Your people, and set their hearts to You"(Divrei Hayamim 29:17-18).

JEALOUSY: The third branch of love [of G-d] is jealousy, namely, that a person be jealous for the sake of His holy Name, hate those who hate Him, and strive to subdue them as much as he can, in order that G-d's service be done and His honor increased.

This is what king David, peace be unto him, said: "O G-d, do I not hate those who hate You? Do I not contend with those who rise up against You? I hate them with an utter hatred; I count them my enemies" (Tehilim 139:21-22). And Eliyahu said: "I have been very jealous for G-d, the L-rd of hosts..." (I Kings 19:10). We already learned what he merited by virtue of his jealousy for G-d, as the Torah states: "because he was jealous for his God and made atonement for the children of Israel" (Bamidbar 25:13).

Our sages, of blessed memory, spoke strongly regarding one who is able to rebuke someone but refrains from doing so. They decreed his judgment to be that he himself will be held accountable for the sin of the sinners. In the Midrash, [they expounded: "'her princes were like deer [that find no pasture...]' (Eicha 1:6) - just like during a heat wave, these deer turn their faces one beneath the other, so too the great sages of Israel would see sin committed and turn their faces away from it. The Holy One, blessed be He, said to them: 'a time will come when I will do the same to them'" (Eicha Raba 1:13).

It is obvious that he who loves his fellow is unable to bear the sight of others beating him or insulting him, and will certainly go out to help him. So too, he who loves the blessed G-d's Name will be unable to bear seeing the desecration of His Name, G-d forbid, and the transgressing of His mitzvot.

This is what Shlomo said: "those who forsake the Torah praise the wicked, but those who keep the Torah contend with them" (Mishlei 28:4). For those who praise the wicked on his wickedness and do not rebuke his deeds to his face, behold, they are the "forsakers of Torah" who abandon it to be desecrated, G-d forbid. But the guardians of the Torah who strengthen themselves to strengthen it, will certainly contend with the wicked and be unable to restrain themselves and be silent. The Holy One, blessed be He, said to Iyov: "Scatter forth the wrath of your anger;

see every arrogant man and submit him; tread down the wicked in their place; press them in the earth together, push their faces in the ground" (Iyov 40:11-13). For this is the intense love that he who truly loves His Creator can demonstrate, and it is written: "those who love G-d hate evil" (Tehilim 97:10).

INTENTION: Thus far, we have clarified the trait of Chasidut as it relates to deeds and manner of performance. We will now explain Chasidut as it relates to intention.

We have already discussed earlier the matter of performing a mitzva "for its own sake" (lishma) and "not for its own sake" (shelo lishma), according to their various levels.

However, he whose motivation in his divine service is to purify his soul before his Creator in order to be worthy of sitting among the Just and the Pious, "to gaze upon the pleasantness of G-d and to dwell within His sanctuary", and receive the reward in the World to Come, we certainly cannot say that his motive is evil.

On the other hand, we also cannot say that this is the best of motives. For as long as a person is motivated by his own benefit, in essence, his divine service is for his own self-interest.

But the true motivation which is found among the Pious, who have exerted themselves and strove to attain it, is for one to serve solely in order to raise and increase the honor of the Master, blessed be He.

This intent will come only after the love of Him has intensified within him, after he longs and lusts for the raising of His honor and is pained by any diminishing of it. For then he will perform the divine service for this purpose, so that at least, through himself, G-d's honor will increase.

He will lust that all other human beings will likewise do the same. And he will be pained and grieve when they diminish in this honor. All the more so, will he be pained of what he himself diminishes, whether accidentally, unwittingly or due to natural weakness, which makes it difficult for him to guard himself from sin at all times, as scripture writes: "for there is no righteous man on earth who does good and sins not" (Kohelet 7:20).

This matter was clarified in Tana D'Bei Eliyahu (Raba 4): "every sage of Israel who has attained true Torah knowledge, and grieves over the honor of the Holy One, blessed be He, and over the honor of Israel all his days, who longs and feels pain for the honor of Jerusalem and the holy Temple, and for the redemption to sprout soon, and the ingathering of the exiles immediately the Ruach Hakodesh will rest upon his words..."

Thus, we learn that this is the ideal intent. For it is completely removed from all consideration of personal benefit, and is only for the honor of G-d and for the sanctification of His blessed Name, which is sanctified by His creations when they do His will.

On this our sages said: "who is Pious (a Chasid)? He who is benevolent (mitchased) towards his Maker" (Zohar Beit, Mishpatim 114b). Behold, such a Chasid, besides the service which he does in performing his mitzvot with the proper intent, will certainly feel actual (mamash) pain on the exile and the destruction of the Temple, because these causes a diminishing, so to speak, of the blessed G-d's honor. He will long for the Redemption because then the honor of G-d will be exulted. This is what the Tana d'Bei Eliyahu we brought earlier said: "and he longs and feels pain over the honor of Jerusalem..." He will pray always for the redemption of Israel and the return of G-d's honor.

If one will say: "who am I, and what importance am I that I should pray on the exile and Jerusalem? Will the exiles be ingathered and the salvation sprout because of my prayers?.

The answer to him is near [his question], as we learned: "Thus man was created alone, so that each person should say: 'for my sake the world was created' " (Sanhedrin 37a). Already it brings gratification to G-d, that His children desire and pray for this. And even though their request may not be fulfilled, because the proper time has not yet come or for some other reason, nevertheless, they have done their part and the Holy One, blessed be He, rejoices in this.

On the absence of this, the prophets complained saying: "And He saw that there was no man, and He was astounded for there was no intercessor"(Yeshaya 59:16) and "I looked, and there was none to help; and I was astonished that there was no one to uphold" (Yeshaya 63:5). And it is stated: "it is Zion; no one inquires after her" (Yirmiyahu 30:17), which our sages expounded: "this implies it needs inquiring after" (Sukkah 41a).

Thus, we learn from here that we are obligated in this matter, and cannot exempt ourselves due to our lack of power. For on all such matters, we learned: "It is not incumbent upon you to complete the task, but neither are you free to abstain from it" (Avot 2:16).

And the prophet further said: "She has none to guide her out of all the sons she bore, none takes her hand of all the sons she raised" (Yeshaya 51:18). And "all flesh is grass, and all his kindness is as the blossom of the field" (Isaiah 40:6), which our sages of blessed memory, explained: "all the kindness they do is only for themselves" (Zohar Chadash 117a, Tikunei Zohar 30,63a), i.e. for their own good and benefit; they do not intend for this perfect intention and do not seek the raising of G-d's honor and the redemption of Israel.

For it is impossible for the honor of G-d to be raised except through the redemption of Israel and the raising of Israel's honor, since in truth, one depends on the other, as the prophet said in Tana D'Bei Eliyahu I mentioned: "and he grieves over the honor of the Holy One, blessed be He, and over the honor of Israel".

Thus, we learn that there are two matters in this. One, that the intention behind every mitzva and act of divine service be the increase in the honor of G-d which comes from His creations' doing what brings gratification to Him. Two, that one feel pain and seeks for the elevation of this honor, which will occur wholly when the honor and good of Israel will be fully raised.

GOOD OF THE GENERATION: There is another primary principle regarding intention in Chasidut, namely, the good of the generation. For, it is proper for every Chasid to be motivated in his deeds for the good of his entire generation, to bring merit to them and to shield them. This is the intent of the verse: "Say of the righteous man that he is good, for they shall eat the fruits of their deeds" (Isaiah 3:10), that all of the generation eats of his fruits.

Likewise, our sages, of blessed memory, expounded (Bava Batra 15a): "'is there a tree there?' (Bamidbar 13:20) - is there a righteous person who shields the generation like a tree".

You will see that this is the will of G-d, that the Pious of Israel bring merit and atone on all the other classes among them. This is what our sages, of blessed memory, said regarding the Lulav and its species: "let these come and atone for these" (Vayikra Raba 30:11).

For the Holy One, blessed be He, does not desire the destruction of the wicked. It is rather a mitzva incumbent on the Pious to strive to bring merit to them and to atone for them.

This intention needs to be included in his divine service and also be an actual part of his prayers, namely, to pray on behalf of his generation, to atone for he who needs atonement, to bring to repentance he who needs to repent, and to plead in defense of his entire generation.

Our sages of blessed memory already expounded on the verse: "I have come because of your words" (Daniel 10:12) - "that Gavriel was not allowed to re-enter behind the heavenly curtain until he had pleaded in defense of Israel" (Yoma 77a). And on Gideon it was said "go in with your might" (Shoftim 6:14) - "because he pleaded in defense of Israel" (Yalkut Shimoni 247:62).

For the Holy One, blessed be He, only loves he who loves Israel, and the more a person's love of Israel increases, the more the Holy One, blessed be He, increases love for him.

These are the true shepherds of Israel, which the Holy One, blessed be He, greatly desired in, who sacrifice themselves for His sheep, seeking and striving for their peace and well-being in all matters, always standing in the breach to pray for them to annul the harsh decrees, and to open for them the gates of blessings.

To what is this analogous? To that of a father who loves no one more than he whom he sees sincerely loves his sons. This is something that human nature can attest to.

And this is the matter behind the Kohen Gadol (high priest) which our sages said: "[the high priests were not without blame as] they should have implored Divine mercy for their generation, which they failed to do" (Makot 11a). Likewise, they said: "there was a case of a man who was eaten by a lion some three miles from the town where Rabbi Yehoshua ben Levi lived and Eliyahu would not appear to the Rabbi for three days on that account" (Makot 11a). See then, that it is a duty incumbent on the Chasidim to plead and exert themselves on behalf of their generation.

We have clarified the primary divisions of Chasidut. Their particulars are given to every pure heart and mind to conduct himself uprightly in them, each matter in its own time, according to the application of these root principles.

Messilat Yesharim

Chapter 20

What now needs explanation is the weighing of this Piety.

This is a very, very primary matter. Know that, in truth, this is the most difficult work in Chasidut due to its great subtlety and because the evil inclination has much entry into this area. Therefore, its danger is enormous. For the evil inclination may convince a person to distance many good things as if they were evil and draw him near to many sins as if they were great mitzvot.

In truth, a person will not be able to succeed in this "weighing" without three requirements:

He must possess a most pure heart, having no other motive than to bring gratification to the blessed G-d, and nothing else besides this whatsoever.

He must examine his deeds very thoroughly and strive to rectify them according to this purpose.

And after all this, he must cast his burden on G-d. For then, it will be said of him: "fortunate is the man whose strength is in You... G-d will not withhold good from those who walk perfectly (b'tamim)"(Tehilim 84:6-12).

If one of these conditions is lacking in him, he will not attain Wholeness (Shlemut), and is very likely to stumble and fall. That is to say, if his intention is not ideal and pure, or if he will be lax in the in-depth examination of what he is capable of examining, or if even after all this, he does not place his trust in his Master, it will be difficult for him not to fall.

But if he guards all three properly, namely, purity (temimut) of thought, examination, and trust - then he will walk securely in truth and no evil will befall him, as Chana said in her prophecy: "He will guard the feet of His pious ones" (Shmuel 2:9), and likewise David said: "He shall not forsake His pious ones; they will be guarded forever" (Tehilim 37:28).

What a person needs to understand is that one should not judge the matters of Chasidut according to their superficial appearance. Rather, one must examine and contemplate the full extent of where the future consequences of the deed leads. For sometimes, the deed itself may appear to be good but since the consequences are evil one must abstain from it. For doing it would not have made him a Chasid but rather a sinner.

Behold the story of Gedalia ben Achikam where it is clear to our eyes that due to his great Chasidut to not judge Yishmael ben Netanya negatively, nor to accept an evil report, he said to Yochanan ben Kareach "you are speaking falsely of Yishmael" (Yirmiyahu 40:16). What resulted from this? He was murdered, the Jews went into exile, and their last ember was extinguished. Scripture attributes the murder of these people as if Gedalyah himself murdered them, as our sages of blessed memory, said (Nida 61a) on the verse: "all the bodies of the men whom he had killed through Gedaliah" (Yirmiyahu 41:9).

The second temple was likewise destroyed due to such incorrectly weighed Chasidut. In the story of Bar Kamtza (Gitin 56a): "the Rabbis thought to offer the blemished animal [of the emperor in order not to offend him]. Said Rabbi Zechariah ben Avkulas to them: 'people will say that blemished animals may be offered on the altar'. They then proposed to kill Bar Kamtza so that he should not go and inform against them, but Rabbi Zechariah ben Avkulas said to them: 'people will say one who makes a blemish on a consecrated animals is to be put to death'".

In the meantime, that wicked man went and informed against Israel to the Roman emperor, who came and destroyed Jerusalem. This is what Rabbi Yochanan meant when he said on this: "through the humility of Rabbi Zechariah ben Avkulas our House has been destroyed, our Temple burnt and we ourselves exiled from our land" (Gitin 56a).

We thus see that, one must not judge the piety of an act by itself alone. Rather, one must view it from all angles that human intellect can foresee before he can truthfully judge whether it is better to do it or to abstain from it.

For instance, the Torah commanded us: "you shall surely rebuke your fellow" (Vayikra 19:17). Very often a person attempts to rebuke sinners at a place or time when his words will not be heeded and he causes them to breach even further in their wickedness, to desecrate the Name of G-d, and to add transgression to their sin. In such cases, the only Chasidut is to keep silent. Thus, our sages, of blessed memory, said: "just like it is a mitzva to say what will be heeded, so too it is a mitzva to not say what will not be heeded" (Yevamot 65b).

To illustrate, obviously, it is proper for every person to arrive early and run to perform a mitzva, striving to be among those occupied in it. However, sometimes this could lead to a dispute, whereby there will be more desecration of the Name of Heaven and shame to the mitzva than honor. In such cases, certainly the Chasid is obligated to abandon the mitzva and not pursue it.

Likewise, our sages, of blessed memory, said regarding the Levites: "because they knew that whoever carries the Ark merits great reward, they abandoned the Shulchan, Menorah and Altars, and all ran to the Ark to gain reward. Then, this person argued saying 'I will carry it from here' and that person argued saying 'I will carry it from here' until they came to lightheadedness and the Divine presence would hit them..." (Midrash Raba 5:1).

Behold, a man is obligated to guard all of the mitzvot in all of their fine details, doing so before any person, whoever it may be, and not be afraid or ashamed before him. Likewise, it is written: "I will also speak of Your testimonies before kings, and will not be ashamed" (Tehilim 119:46). And we also learned "be brazen as a leopard..." (Avot 5:2).

But, here too one needs to discern and make distinctions, for all this was said regarding the mitzvot themselves which we are completely obligated in. In those one should "set his face like flint" (Isaiah 50:7).

But there are some additional matters of Piety, which if a person were to do before the common people, they will laugh at him and ridicule him, thereby sinning and incurring punishment through him, and this is something he could have abstained from doing since these things are not complete obligations. Thus, for such things, it is certainly more proper for the Chasid to abstain from it than to do it. This is what scripture says: "and walk discreetly with your G-d" (Michah 6:8). Many great Chasidim abstained from their pious practices when in the presence of the common masses because it appears like arrogance.

The general principle: whatever is essential in the mitzva, should be done before all mockers. But whatever is not essential and causes laughter and ridicule, one should not do.

Thus, we learn, that one who aspires to true Piety must weigh all of his deeds according to their consequences and circumstances, namely, their times, company, subject, and place. If abstaining leads to more sanctification of the Name of Heaven and gratification to G-d than doing it, he should abstain and not do it.

Or, if a deed appears good but its consequences or circumstances are bad, or if a deed appears bad but its consequences are good - everything should be decided by the final outcome and consequences, the true fruit of the deed.

These things can only be evaluated by one of understanding heart and sound intellect since it is impossible to clarify all their endless details, and "G-d gives wisdom; from His mouth comes knowledge and understanding" (Mishlei 2:6).

The story involving Rabbi Tarfon illustrates this, for even though he was being stringent on himself to recline like the view of Beit Shammai, he was told by the sages: "you deserved to be liable for having caused your own death, for you transgressed the view of Beit Hillel!" (Berachot 10b).

This is because the Halachic dispute between Beit Shammait and Beit Hillel had become a grave matter in Israel due to the great disputes which grew out from it, and the Halacha had finally been ruled to be as Beit Hillel.

Thus, it had become necessary for the preservation of Torah that this ruling forever remain in full strength and never be weakened, so that the Torah does not, G-d forbid, become like two Torahs. Therefore, according to that Mishna, to adopt the view of Beit Hillel, even when it was lenient, is a greater act of Piety, than to adopt the view of Beit Shammai, even though it was more stringent. Thus, this serves as a guide for us, to discern which path leads to the light of truth and faith, to do what is just in the eyes of G-d.

Messilat Yesharim

Chapter 21

That which will help greatly in acquiring Chasidut is great observation and much contemplation. For when a person contemplates much on G-d's great exaltedness, blessed be He, and His absolute perfection, and the immeasurably great distance between His greatness and our lowliness, he will be filled with fear and trembling before Him.

And when he contemplates G-d's great lovingkindness to us, His great love for the Jewish people, the closeness of the Just to Him, the virtue of Torah and mitzvot, and other similar investigations and studies, certainly, a powerful love will ignite within him, and he will choose and lust to cling to Him. For when he sees that the Creator, blessed be He, is literally (mamash) like a father to us, and has mercy on us as a father on his sons, there will then awaken within him a desire and longing to reciprocate back to Him, as a son to his father.

For this, a person must seclude himself in his chambers, and focus all his knowledge and thought to the observation and in-depth study of these true matters.

That which will certainly help him in this is great diligence and in-depth study of the psalms of David, peace be unto him, contemplating their words and matters. For in their all being full of love and fear [of G-d] and all types of Chasidut, behold, in contemplating them, one cannot help not being greatly inspired to go out in his footsteps and to walk in his ways. Likewise, reading the stories of the Chasidim who followed in these ways will also help in this. For all these things awaken the intellect to take counsel and to do like their noble deeds. This is clear.

The detriments to Chasidut are distractions and worries. For when one's mind is distracted and dispersed with its worries and occupations, it is impossible to turn to this contemplation; and without this contemplation, he will not attain Chasidut. And even if he has already attained it, the distractions force his mind (to attend to them) and confound it, not allowing him to strengthen in fear and love and other matters I mentioned pertaining to Chasidut. Therefore, our sages, of blessed memory, said: "the divine presence does not rest through sadness..." (Shabbat 30b).

And all the more so [does this apply] to the [physical] pleasures and indulgences which are verily (mamash) the opposite of Chasidut. For, behold, they seduce the heart to be drawn after them, and to veer away from all matters of Separation and true knowledge.

However, that which can protect a person and save him from these detriments is trust in G-d. Namely, that a person casts his burden entirely upon G-d, knowing that it is certainly impossible for a man to lack what was designated for him, as our sages taught: "all of a person's sustenance [for the year] is fixed for him from Rosh Hashana [to Yom Kippur]" (Beitzah 16a). Likewise, they said: "no man can touch what was prepared for his fellow even to the extent of a hair's breadth" (Yomah 38b).

A person could have sat idle and the decree would have been fulfilled (his designated portion would have come to him), had it not been preceded by the fine imposed on every human being: "by the sweat of your brow shall you eat bread" (Gen.3:19), whereby a person is required to make some effort for obtaining his livelihood, for thus the exalted King decreed.

This is like a tax imposed on the human race which one cannot escape from paying. Therefore, our sages, of blessed memory, said (Sifri 15:18): "I might think one can sit idle, but scripture says (Devarim 28:20): 'in all that you set your hand to do' ".

Only that it is not the efforts (hishtadlut) that help. Rather, the efforts are necessary, but once one has put in some effort, he has already discharged his obligation and there is place for the blessing of Heaven to rest upon him, and he need not consume his days in exertion and labor. This is what king David said: "For not from the east or from the west, nor from... but it is G-d who executes judgment, [putting down one and lifting up another]" (Tehilim 75:7-8), and king Shlomo said: "Do not weary yourself to grow rich; cease applying your understanding" (Mishlei 23:4).

Rather, the true path is that of the "early Pious ones", who made their Torah primary and their work secondary, and succeeded in both (Berachot 35b). For once a man does a little work, from then on, he need only trust in his Master, and not be distressed by any worldly matters. Then his mind will be free and his heart ready for true Chasidut and perfect divine service.

Messilat Yesharim

Chapter 22

We already spoke earlier on the disgrace of arrogance, and by inference, we learned on the praiseworthiness of Humility. Let us now explain Humility in a more fundamental manner and arrogance will become clarified by itself.

The general matter of Humility is for a person not to attribute importance to himself for any reason whatsoever. This is the exact opposite of arrogance and the effects that result from this are the opposite of those that result from arrogance.

When we examine closely, we will find that Humility is dependent both on thought and deed. For at first, a person needs to become humble in his thoughts and only afterwards, can he conduct himself in the ways of the Humble.

This is because, if he is not yet humble in his thoughts and he wishes to be humble in his deeds, he will only become as one of the deceitful and evil "humble" men we mentioned earlier (ch.11), who belong to the class of hypocrites, the worst kind of evil men to be found in the world. Let us now explain these divisions.

Humility in thought is for a person to contemplate and come to realize as truth that he is undeserving of praise and honor, and all the more so [unworthy] of being elevated over his fellow men. This is due to what he lacks and also to what [good] he has actually attained.

Due to what he lacks: this is evident, for it is impossible for a man, whatever level of perfection he may have reached, to not have many deficiencies, whether due to his nature, or due to his family and relatives, due to certain events that happened to him, or due to his own deeds. For "there is no righteous man on earth who does good and sins not" (Kohelet 7:20). All these are blemishes on a person which allow him no room whatsoever to become haughty. Even if he has attained many virtues, nevertheless these deficiencies are enough to obscure them.

That which most brings a person to pride and arrogance is wisdom. For wisdom is a quality in a man himself, in his most noble faculty, namely, his intellect.

But there is no sage that will not make mistakes and that will not need to learn from the words of his peers, and very often, even from his students. How then can he pride himself on his wisdom?

One who possesses a straight intellect, even if he has merited to become a great sage and truly distinguished, when he looks and contemplates, will see that there is no room for haughtiness and pride. For behold, he who possesses high intelligence, who knows more than others, merely does what it is his nature to do. He is like a bird which flies upwards because of its nature, or an ox which pulls with its might because of its nature. So too for he who is wise. This is because his nature brings him to this. But for another person who is currently not as wise as him, if he had possessed natural intelligence like him, would also have become just as wise. Hence, there is no room to elevate and pride oneself in this.

Rather, if he possesses great wisdom, behold, he is under duty to teach it to those in need of it, similar to the statement of Rabbi Yochanan ben Zakai: "if you learned much Torah, do not take credit for yourself since for this you were created!" (Avot 2:8).

If he is wealthy, he may rejoice in his lot, but it is incumbent upon him to help those who do not have. If he is strong, he must help those who are weak and rescue the oppressed.

To what is this similar? To servants in a household where each one is charged with a matter and it is incumbent on each to stand on his appointed position to uphold the affairs and needs of the house. In truth, there is no place for pride here.

Behold, this is the type of examination and contemplation proper for every person whose intellect is straight and not perverse. When this will become clear to him, he may be called a truly humble person, for he is humble in his heart and inner being. This is as David said to Michal: "I was lowly in my own eyes" (Shmuel II 6:22).

Our sages, of blessed memory, said (Sotah 5b): "Rabbi Yehoshua ben Levi said: Come and see how great are the lowly of spirit, for when the Temple stood, a man brought a burnt-offering and earned the reward of a burnt-offering, a flour-offering and he earned the reward of a flour-offering; but as for him whose mind is lowly, Scripture ascribes it to him as though he had offered every one of the sacrifices; as it is said: The sacrifices of G-d are a broken spirit."

Behold, this is a praise of the lowly of spirit, who are humble in heart and in thought.

They further said (Chulin 89a): "'It was not because you were greater than any people that the L-rd desired in you and chose you' (Devarim 7:7) - the Holy One, blessed be He, said to Israel, 'My sons, I desire you because even when I bestow greatness upon you, you humble yourselves before Me. I bestowed greatness upon Avraham, yet he said to Me, 'I am but dust and ashes' (Gen.18:27); Upon Moses and Aharon, yet they said: 'And we are nothing' (Ex.16:7); upon David, yet he said: 'I am but a worm and no man' (Tehilim 22:7)"

All this because the man possessing a just heart does not allow himself to become seduced by any virtue which he comes to. This is due to truly knowing that because of this virtue, he does not emerge out of his lowliness, due to other defects inevitably within him. And furthermore, even in those mitzvot themselves which he attained, he certainly has not arrived at their ultimate goal.

Furthermore still, even if he had no other deficiency than of being flesh and blood, born of woman, this would be more than enough of a lowliness and inferiority, so that he will not find it at all befitting to pride himself. For any virtue he attains is nothing but a kindness of G-d on him, who wants to favor him despite that by his nature and physicality, he is extremely lowly and insignificant. Therefore, he must only thank He who is so gracious towards him and always humble himself more and more.

To what is this analogous? To a destitute pauper who receives gifts as a kindliness and cannot help not feeling shame. The more kindness he receives, the more shame he feels. So too is this matter analogous to every man whose eyes are opened and can see himself, when he attains virtues from G-d, blessed be He. This is as king David said: "what shall I repay G-d for all His kindliness to me?" (Tehilim 116:12).

We have already learned about some men of great piety who, despite all of their piety, were punished for attributing credit to themselves.

On Nechemia ben Chachalya our sages, of blessed memory, said: "why was his book not called by his name? Because he claimed credit for himself" (Sanhedrin 93b).

Likewise Chizkiyahu said: "to peace it is bitterness for me" (Isaiah 38:17) since the Holy One, blessed be He, answered him: "I will defend this city to save it, for My sake and for the sake of My servant David" (Isaiah 37:35). This is as the statement of our sages: "whoever makes his request depend on his own merit, is shown that it was dependent on the merit of others" (Berachot 10b).

This demonstrates that a person should not even take credit on his good deeds. How much more so, should he not feel proud and haughty for them.

However, all this is what is proper to set in one's heart for he who would be like Avraham, like Moshe, like Aharon, like David, and the other Chasidim we have mentioned.

But as for us who are orphans of orphans, we do not need all of this, for we have such an abundance of deficiencies. One does not need a great examination to see our lowliness and to realize that all of our wisdom is considered as nothing.

For the greatest sage among us is no greater than one of the disciples of the disciples of the early generations. It is proper for us to truly understand and know this, so that our hearts should not become proud for nothing. Rather, we must realize that our understanding and intellect is extremely weak. Foolishness is strong by us and error is prevalent. What knowledge we possess is but a tiny bit of a tiny bit. Hence, certainly it is not proper for us to pride ourselves in the least but rather to feel shame and lowliness. This is obvious.

HUMILITY OF DEED: We have spoken until now on Humility of thought. We will now speak on Humility of deed. This area divides into four parts: conducting oneself in lowliness, bearing insults, hating Rabbanut (authority over others) and fleeing honor, and granting honor to everyone.

Conducting oneself in lowliness: it is proper for this to be in one's speaking, walking, sitting and all of one's movements.

In one's speaking: our sages, of blessed memory, said: "one should always speak with other people in a gentle manner" (Yomah 86a). This is stated explicitly in scripture: "the words of the wise are heeded [when spoken] gently" (Kohelet 9:17). One's words should be of honoring [others] not of belittling them. Likewise scripture says: "he who belittles his fellow lacks sense" (Mishlei 11:12), and "when the wicked comes, there also comes contempt" (Mishlei 18:3).

In one's walking: Our sages, of blessed memory, said: "They sent word from Israel. Who is destined for the world to come? He who is meek, humble, stooping on entering and on going out" (Sanhedrin 88b).

One must not walk in an overly erect posture nor with excessive heaviness, heel to toe, rather as one going to his occupations. Likewise our sages, of blessed memory, said: "If one walks with an overly erect posture even for four cubits, it is as if he pushes against the feet of the Divine Presence" (Berachot 43b), and it is written: "and those of lofty height will be cut down" (Isaiah 10:33).

In one's sitting: that one's place be among the lowly and not among the prominent. This is likewise stated explicitly in scripture: "Do not glorify yourself before a king, and do not stand in the place of great men; for it is better that he say to you, 'Come up here', than to humble you before a prince..." (Mishlei 25:6-7). Likewise, our sages of blessed memory said: "distance two or three places from your [proper] place and sit until you are told 'come forward!', rather than to go up until they tell you 'move back!'" (Vayikra Raba 1:5).

Regarding those who diminish themselves, our sages of blessed memory, said: "whoever diminishes himself for the sake of Torah in this world is made great in the World to Come" (Bava Metzia 85b).

And corresponding to this they said (Yalkut Shimoni Yechezkel 361): "'[So said the L-rd G-d:] I shall remove the turban and lift off the crown [the humble will be uplifted, and the high will be humbled]' (Yechezkel 21:31) - whoever is great in this world will be small in the World to Come". We also learn the opposite: if one is small in this world, his time of greatness will be in the World to Come.

And our sages of blessed memory said: "Man should always learn from the mind of his Creator; for behold, the Holy One, blessed be He, ignored all the mountains and heights and caused His Shechinah to abide upon Mount Sinai" (Sotah 5a). This was because of Mount Sinai's lowliness.

Likewise, they said: "'for the remnant of His inheritance' (Michah 7:18) - for him who makes himself a mere remnant" (Rosh Hashana 17b).

BEARING INSULTS: The second division of humility is in bearing insults. Behold, our sages, of blessed memory, explicitly said: "Who is forgiven iniquity? He who overlooks transgression" (Rosh Hashana 17b).

They further said (Shabbat 88b): "Those who are insulted but do not insult back, hear themselves insulted but do not answer back... of them scripture says: 'But they who love Him shall be as the sun when it goes forth in its might' (Shoftim 5:31) ".

Our sages told us about the great humility of Bava ben Buta saying:

"A certain Babylonian went up to Israel and took a wife [there]. 'Cook for me two hooves', he requested, [misunderstanding his language] she boiled him two lentils, which made him angry. The next day he said, 'Boil me a lot', so she boiled him a huge amount. 'Go and bring me two small pumpkins'. so, she went and brought him two candles. 'Go and break them on the head of the Baba (threshold)... so, she went and broke them on the head of Baba ben Buta. He said to her, 'What is the meaning of what you have done?' - She replied, 'Thus my husband commanded me.' He said to her: 'You have fulfilled your husband's will, may the Almighty grant you two sons like Baba ben Buta" (Nedarim 66b).

Likewise, our sages told us about the great humility of Hillel saying: "Our Rabbis taught: A man should always be humble like Hillel..." (Shabbat 30b).

Likewise Rabbi Abahu, despite his great humility, found that he had not yet reached the point where he may be fittingly called a humble person, as our sages told: "Rabbi Abahu said: At first I used to think that I was humble; but when I saw R. Abba of Akko offer one explanation and his interpreter offer another [to the audience] and he was not bothered, I considered that I was not humble" (Sotah 40a).

HATING RABBANUT: Hating Rabbanut (authority over others) and fleeing from honor: This is an explicit Mishna (Avot 1:10): "love work, hate Rabbanut". They further said: "One whose heart is frivolous in handing down rulings is a fool, wicked and arrogant" (Avot 4:7), and "whoever chases after honor, honor flees from him" (Eruvin 13b), and "'Do not go out quickly to quarrel (Riv)' (Mishlei 25:8) - do not run after rulership, Why not? [the verse continues:] 'for what will you do in the end' (ibid), the next day people will put questions to you, and what will you answer them?" (Pesikta Rabati 22:4);

Also, there "Rabbi Menachem in the name of Rabbi Tanchum: 'whoever takes on himself a position of authority in order to derive benefit from it, is like an adulterer who derives pleasure from the body of a woman".

Also, there "I (G-d) am called 'holy', thus if you do not possess all of My traits, do not accept a position of rulership upon yourself!".

The disciples of Raban Gamliel demonstrate this, for they were in financial need due to poverty and nevertheless did not want to accept a position of rulership. This is what was stated in the chapter "Kohen Mashuach": (Horayot 10a): "Do you imagine that I offer you rulership? It is servitude that I offer you!".

They further said: "Woe to rulership for it buries (slays) its possessor" (Pesachim 87b). From where do we learn this? From Yosef, for because he conducted himself in rulership, died before his brothers (Berachot 55a).

The general principle in the matter: Rabbanut is nothing but a heavy burden on the shoulders of its bearer. For as long as a man is sitting alone in his house, merely a part of humanity, he is held accountable only for himself. But once he assumed a position of Rabbanut and dominion, already he is held accountable for every person under his authority because it is incumbent on him to watch over all of them, pasture them with knowledge and understanding, and straighten their deeds. If he does not do so, our sages declared - "their sins are inscribed on your head"(Midrash Devarim Rabba 1:13).

HONOR: Honor is nothing but vanity of vanities. It forces a person to act against his will and against the will of his Maker, and to forget all of his duties. He who recognizes it will certainly abhor and hate honor. The praises which other people call him will be a burden on him. For when he sees them heaping praises on what he in truth does not possess, he only feels embarrassment, sighing not only on the evil that he lacks these virtues, but also in that they burden on him false praises in order to humiliate him even more.

HONORING OTHERS: The fourth division is granting honor to every person. Likewise, we learned "who is honorable? He who honors the public" (Avot 4:1). They further said: "from where do we know that a person who knows that his neighbor is greater than himself in even one respect must show him honor..." (Pesachim 113b).

We also learned: "'be first to greet every man' (Avot 4:15) - our sages reported of Rabbi Yochanan ben Zakai that no man ever preceded greeting him, not even a gentile in the marketplace" (Berachot 17a).

One is under duty to grant honor to his fellow men, whether in speech or in deed. Our sages, of blessed memory, already told us about the 24,000 disciples of Rabbi Akiva who died because they did not grant honor to each other (Yevamot 62b).

Just as contempt is associated with the wicked, as in the verse we mentioned earlier "When a wicked man comes, there also comes contempt" (Mishlei 18:3), so is honor associated with the righteous. For honor resides with them and does not separate from them, and it is written: "and before his elders there is honor"(Isaiah 24:23).

We have explained the main divisions of humility. Their particulars are like all other such matters which expand and branch out depending on the times, places, and circumstances - "let the wise man hear and increase understanding" (Mishlei 1:5).

There is no doubt that humility removes many stumbling blocks from a man's path and draws him near to many good things. For the humble person will be little concerned with worldly matters and not envy its vanities. Furthermore, the company of a humble person is extremely pleasant and the public derives pleasure from him. Perforce he will not come to anger and disputes. Rather he does everything quietly and tranquilly. Fortunate is he who has merited this trait. Our sages, of blessed memory, already said: "that which wisdom made a crown on its head, humility made as the heel of its sandal" (Yerushalmi Shabbat 1:3), for all wisdom cannot compare to it. This is clear.

Messilat Yesharim

Chapter 23

The are two things that habituate a person to Humility: habit and contemplation.

Habit: that a person habituate himself slowly, slowly to conduct himself in lowliness, in the manner we discussed previously, to sit in lower places, to walk at the rear of the group, to wear modest clothing, namely, clothing that is dignified but not glorious. When a person habituates himself in this manner, slowly, slowly, humility will enter in his heart until it will be implanted properly.

Since the nature of a man's heart is to become proud and haughty, it is difficult for him to root out this natural tendency at its source. But by performing external actions that are under his control, he will slowly, slowly draw in his inner being the matter which is not so much in his control. This is similar to what we wrote in Zeal. All this is included in the statement of our sages, of blessed memory, "a man should always be cunning in the fear of heaven" (Berachot 17a), namely, that one seeks out strategies to employ against his nature and tendencies until he vanquishes them.

The contemplation, however, is on various matters. One of them is brought in the statement of Akavia ben Mehalelel: "know from where you came - from a putrid drop; and where you are going - to a place of dirt, worms, and maggots; and before whom you are destined to give a judgment and accounting - before the supreme King of kings, the Holy One, blessed be He" (Avot 3:1).

For in truth, all these thoughts are counter to arrogance and they foster humility, because when a man looks at the lowliness of his physicality and the baseness of his origin, he will have no reason whatsoever to be haughty but only to feel shame and humiliation.

To what is this similar? To a pig-herder who rose to become the king. As long as he remembers his early days, it will be impossible for him to become arrogant. Likewise, when one considers that at the end of all his greatness, he will return to the earth to be food for maggots, all the more so will his pride be submitted and his roaring arrogance quieted. For what is his good and his greatness if his end is shame and dishonor?

And when he contemplates further and pictures in his mind the moment he enters before the great Beit Din of the heavenly host, when he finds himself before the King of kings, the Holy One, blessed be He, who is absolutely pure and holy, in the midst of the assembly of holy ones, mighty servants, strong in power, obeying His word, without any blemish whatsoever, and he stands before them, base, lowly, and petty in and of himself, defiled and polluted due to his deeds. Will he then raise his head? Will he have what to answer? And when they ask him: "where has your mouth gone? Where is the pride and honor which you assumed in your world?"

What will he answer? What will he reply to this rebuke? Behold, certainly if for one moment, a person were to visualize in his mind this truth with a true and strong picture, all of his arrogance would blast off in flight, never to return.

The second contemplation is on the shifting of circumstances over time and their many changes. For the rich man may easily become poor, the ruler a slave, the honorable lowly. If one can so easily fall to a situation which is today disgraceful in his eyes, how can his heart pride on his current situation in which he is not assured of?! How many kinds of illnesses can, G-d forbid, strike a person which would necessitate him to plea others to help him and assist him to relieve his situation a bit. How many troubles can befall him such that he would need to beseech many people to save him when previously he sometimes despised to greet them?

These are things we see with our own eyes on a daily basis. They are enough to remove arrogance from a man's heart and clothe him with humility and lowliness.

And when a man contemplates further on his obligation to G-d, blessed be He, and to what extent it is neglected by him and how much he is lax in it, certainly he will feel shame and not arrogance, humiliation and not elevation of heart. Likewise, scripture says: "I have indeed heard Ephraim grieving... for after my repentance I have regretted; and after I realized, I smote my thigh; I felt ashamed and disgraced" (Yirmiyahu 31:17-18).

Above all, one should always contemplate to recognize the weakness of human intellect and its great many errors and falsehoods, how it is always nearer to error than true knowledge. Therefore, he should always fear this danger, and seek to learn from every person, always listening to advice, lest he stumble. This is what our sages, of blessed memory, said: "Who is wise? He who learns from all men" (Avot 4:1), and scripture says "he who hearkens to counsel is wise" (Mishlei 12:15).

The detriments of this trait are abundance and satiation in the good of this world, similar to what scripture states explicitly: "lest when you have eaten and become sated [and built good houses...] and your heart grows haughty..." (Devarim 8:12-14).

Therefore the pious deemed it good for a man to afflict himself sometimes, in order to put down the evil inclination of arrogance, which grows strong only through abundance, similar to what our sages, of blessed memory, said: "a lion does not roar over a basket of straw but over a basket of meat" (Berachot 32a).

At the head of all the detriments to humility is foolishness and lack of true knowledge. You can observe that arrogance is found most prevalently among those who are most foolish.

And our sages, of blessed memory, said "a sign of arrogance is poverty of Torah" (Sanhedrin 24a). And likewise they said: "a sign of not knowing anything is self-praise" (Zohar Balak 49b); and "one coin in a pitcher cries out 'rattle, rattle'" (Bava Metzia 85b); and "the barren trees were asked: 'why are your voices heard?' they replied: 'would that it were that our voices will be heard and we will be remembered'" (Bereishis Raba 16:3).

We have already seen that Moses, the greatest man that ever lived, was also the most humble.

Another of the detriments of humility is associating with or being served by flatterers, who try to steal a person's heart with their flattery in order to benefit themselves. They will praise and exalt him by exaggerating to the extreme whatever virtues he possesses and by adding to this, virtues he does not at all possess. Sometimes what he does possess is the very opposite of what they praise him for.

The end of the matter is that a man is light-minded, his nature is weak, and he is easily seduced. This is especially so for something to which his nature inclines. Therefore when he hears these things said by someone he trusts, it will enter into him like the venom of a snake and he falls into the net of pride and becomes broken.

For example, we see by Yoash [ben Achazya king of Judah] (Shemot Raba 8:2) who acted good all the days he was taught by his teacher Yehoyada HaKohen. But after the death of Yehoyada, his servants came and began to flatter him and magnify praises of him until they likened him to a god; "Then the king hearkened to them" (Divrei Hayamim II 24:17).

You can see clearly that most high officials and kings or other people in positions of power, regardless of their rank, stumble and become corrupted by the flattery of their subordinates.

Therefore, he whose eyes are on his head (Kohelet 2:14), should be more watchful to scrutinize the deeds of someone who he wishes to acquire as a friend, advisor, or workers over his household than he is watchful to scrutinize his food and drink. For his food and drink can only damage his body while his friends and workers can destroy his soul, belongings and all of his honor. King David peace be unto him said: "He will not dwell within my house, he who practices deceit. He who follows the way of the innocent, he will serve me" (Tehilim 101:6-7).

The only good then is for a person to seek out honest friends who will enlighten his eyes to what he is blind and will rebuke him out of love, thus rescuing him from all evil. For what a man cannot see due to his inability to see fault with himself, they will see and understand and warn him, and he will be protected. On this scripture says: "in abundance of counselors there is salvation"(Mishlei 24:6).

Messulat Chapter 23 Yesharim

Messilat Yesharim

Chapter 24

Noting that this trait was counted after all the virtuous traits we mentioned until now is enough to awaken us to its [lofty] matter. Certainly, it must be an important and fundamental matter and difficult to attain. For it can be reached only by one who has already acquired all of the previously mentioned traits.

However, we must first introduce that there are two types of fear which are effectively three types. The first type is very easy to attain, there being nothing easier. The second is difficult, while the second part of the second type, is more difficult than everything.

Its perfection is likewise, a very great form of perfection. The first type is fear of punishment, and the second is fear of G-d's exaltedness (Yirat Haromemut), of which Fear of Sin is the second part therein. We will now explain their matters and differences.

Fear of punishment, as its name implies, is for a person to fear transgressing the word of the L-rd, his G-d, due to the punishments incurred for the transgression, whether to body or soul. This [type of fear] is certainly easy to attain. For every man loves himself and fears for his soul and there is nothing which keeps a person from doing something more than the fear that this thing might bring harm to him.

But this type of fear is befitting only to the ignorant and women, who are light-minded. But it is not the fear of the sages and the men of knowledge.

The second type of fear is fear of G-d's exaltedness (Yirat Haromemut). It means that a person distances and refrains from sin because of G-d's great honor, blessed be His Name. For how could his heart of flesh and blood, lowly and petty, allow or dare do something against the will of the Creator, blessed and exalted be His Name?!

This type of fear is not so easy to attain, for it will arise only out of knowledge and thought, [namely] by contemplating G-d's exaltedness, blessed be He, and the lowliness of man. All these things are outgrowths of the intellect which understands and attains insight. This is the fear we described previously in Piety, setting it as the second part of one of the divisions of Piety.

When experiencing this fear [of G-d's exaltedness], a person will feel shame and tremble when standing before his Maker to pray or when performing any divine service. This is the praiseworthy fear which the pious great men were praised for. It is what Moshe referred to when he said: "to fear this glorious and awesome Name, the L-rd, your G-d" (Devarim 28:58).

The Fear of Sin, which we are here explaining, is like a branch of the "Fear of G-d's exaltedness" (yirat haromemut) mentioned above, but also like a separate, independent type of fear. It is matter is for a man to constantly fear and worry on his deeds lest some impurity or sin mix in with them, or lest there be some matter, small or big, which is not befitting G-d's great honor, and His exalted Name.

You can see the close relationship between this fear and the "Fear of G-d's exaltedness" we mentioned. For the aim of both is for one to not do something contrary to G-d's exalted honor, blessed be He.

But the distinction between them for which Fear of Sin is considered a separate type and called by a different name is that "Fear of G-d's Exaltedness" is only during performance of a deed, during divine service or during refraining from sin, namely, at the time one stands in prayer or engages in divine service, that he should feel ashamed and abashed, tremble and quake before G-d's exalted honor, blessed be He; or at the time an opportunity to commit a sin presents itself before him, and he recognizes that it is a sin, that he refrains from doing it in order to not do something to provoke the eyes of His glory, G-d forbid.

But "Fear of Sin" is at all times and moments. At every moment he is afraid, lest he stumble and does something or half-something which will be against the honor of His Name, blessed be He.

This is why it is called "fear of sin", for its primary matter is fear of sin (not G-d), that it not enters and mix in his deeds due to some negligence or laxness or due to forgetfulness for whatever reason. On this it was said: "Fortunate is the man that fears always" (Mishlei 28:14), which our sages of blessed memory explained: "that verse refers to words of Torah" (Berachot 60a). For even when one does not see a stumbling block before his eyes, his heart must feel dread within lest there be one hidden at his feet and he did not guard [from it].

On this fear Moshe Rabeinu, peace be unto him, said: "in order that His fear shall be upon your faces, so that you shall not sin" (Shmot 20:17). For this is the primary fear - that a man fear and tremble always until this fear never leaves Him. For through this, certainly, he will not come to sin, and if he does come to sin, it will be considered as accidental. Isaiah said in his prophecy: "this is the one to whom I will look: he who is humble and contrite in spirit and trembles at my word" (Isaiah 66:2). And king David extolled in this: "Princes have pursued me for nothing, but my heart feared [only] Your word" (Tehilim 119:161).

We have already found that the great and lofty angels, tremble and quake constantly due to the exaltedness of G-d. Our sages, of blessed memory, said in their wise analogies: "from where does the Dinur river (of fire) spring forth? From the sweat of the Chayot (angels)" (Chagigah 13b).

This is because of the dread these lofty angels constantly experience of G-d's exaltedness, blessed be He, lest they detract a small amount from the honor and holiness due before His presence. Whenever and on whatever place the divine presence reveals itself, there is agitation, trembling, and quaking. This is what scripture refers to saying: "The earth trembled, the heavens also dropped at the presence of G-d" (Tehilim 68:9), and "had You rent the heavens, had You descended, mountains would have melted from before You" (Isaiah 63:19).

How much more so is it proper for human beings to tremble and quake, realizing that they are always before G-d, and that they may easily do something which is not befitting His exalted honor, blessed be His Name.

This is what Eliphaz said to Iyov: "What is man that he would be pure, and that one born of woman should be found righteous? Lo! He does not believe in His holy ones, and the heavens are not pure in His eyes" (Iyov 15:14-15), and "Behold, in His servants he puts no trust, and his angels he charges with error; how much more those who dwell in houses of clay, whose foundation is in the dust, who are crushed before the worm" (ibid 18:19). Therefore, behold, certainly every human being should always fear and quake, as Elihu said: "At this also my heart quakes and leaps out from its place; Hear attentively the thunder of His voice and the rumbling that emanates from His mouth" (Iyov 37:1-2).

This is the true fear which should always be upon the face of the pious man and never leave him.

However, there are two divisions of this fear: the first relates to the present or future and the second to the past.

For the present: that a man fear and worry always on what he is presently doing or about to do lest there may enter something which is not in accordance with His honor, as we mentioned earlier.

For the past: that a man always reflects on what he already did, fearing and worrying, lest some sin unknowingly went out through his hands.

This is as the matter of Bava Ben Buta who would bring an Asham Talui (undetermined guilt offering) every day (Keritut 25a). Likewise, Iyov, after his sons' feast, would rise early and bring burnt offerings according to the number of them all. For he told himself: "perhaps my children have sinned [and blasphemed G-d in their hearts]" (Iyov 1:5).

And our sages of blessed memory said of Moshe and Aharon regarding the "anointment oil" with which Moshe anointed Aharon, that they feared perhaps they would transgress somehow by using it unlike its commandment, for it was stated "It shall not be poured upon the flesh of a man" (Shemot 30:32). Thus, our sages said (Horayot 12a):

"Concerning this matter, Moshe worried and said, 'perhaps I have, G-d forbid, made a profane use of the anointing oil?' A heavenly voice came forth and called out, 'as the precious oil on the head descends on the beard of Aharon.., as the dew of Hermon' (Tehilim 133:2-3), just as the law of profane use of holy objects is not applicable to the dew of Hermon, so also there was no profane use of the anointing oil on the beard of Aharon. Aaron however, was still worried. He said, 'It may be that Moshe did not transgress, but perhaps I have transgressed'. Another heavenly voice came forth and said to him, 'Behold how good and how pleasant it is for brothers to dwell together' (Tehilim 133:1) - as Moshe is not guilty of profane use, so are you not guilty of profane use".

Thus, we see that it is the way of the pious, that even in the mitzvot they perform, they worry and say to themselves: "perhaps there was mixed in them some trace of impurity, G-d forbid".

Avraham: after he went out to assist his nephew Lot who had been taken captive, was afraid and told himself perhaps his deeds were not completely pure, as our sages explained on the verse: "do not fear Avraham" (Gen.15:1) - "Rabbi Levi said: 'because Avraham was afraid and said to himself, among all those soldiers I killed in battle, perhaps there was among them a righteous or G-d fearing person?'. Therefore, he was told (Gen.15:1): 'do not fear Avraham'" (Genesis Raba 44:4). And our sages said in Tana D'Bei Eliyahu (Rabba 25): "a person is not told 'do not fear' unless he is G-d fearing in truth".

That is, this true fear which our sages said of it: "The Holy One, blessed be He, has nothing in His world except a treasury of fear of heaven" (Berachot 33b). Only for Moshe was it easy to attain due to his great clinging to G-d, blessed be He. But to other people, certainly the physical is a powerful impediment within them. However, it is proper for every Chasid to exert himself to attain of it all that he is capable, and it is written: "Fear the L-rd, His holy ones" (Tehilim 34:10).

Messilat Yesharim

Chapter 25

The way to acquire this type of fear is through contemplation on two true matters:

One, that the Divine presence (Shechina), blessed be He, is found in every place in the world and [two] that G-d watches over all things, small or great. Nothing is hidden from His sight, neither due to its greatness nor due to its smallness. Rather the great matter and the small matter, the lowly and the honorable, He sees and understands without any distinction.

This is what scripture says: "the whole earth is full of His glory" (Isaiah 6:3), and "Do I not fill heaven and earth?" (Yirmiyahu 23:24), and "Who is like the L-rd, our G-d, enthroned on high, who stoops to look down on the heavens and the earth?" (Tehilim 113:5-6), and "though the L-rd is high, yet He sees the lowly, and the proud He knows from afar" (Tehilim 138:6).

Once it has become clear to a person that wherever he is, he is standing before the Divine Presence, blessed be He, then the fear will come of itself and the dread lest he stumble in his actions, such that they are not befitting of His exalted honor.

This is what our sages said: "Know what is above you: an eye that sees, an ear that hears, and all your deeds are inscribed in a book" (Avot 2:1). For since the Holy One, blessed be He, watches over every thing, and He sees everything and hears everything, certainly every action will leave an impression. And all of them are inscribed in a book, whether for merit or for debt (punishment).

However, this picture is not formed well in a person's mind, except through diligent contemplation and great reflection. For since the matter is far from our senses, the mind can only picture it after much thought and consideration. And even after the mind pictures it, the picture will easily be lost unless he is very diligent in [maintaining] it.

Thus, we see that just like much contemplation is the way to acquire constant fear, so too interruption of thought and idleness of study is its greatest detriment, whether this is due to preoccupations or will - every interruption of thought is a nullification of the constant fear.

This is what the Holy One, blessed be He, commanded the king: "And the Torah shall be with him, and he shall read it all the days of his life, so that he will learn to fear the L-rd, his G-d" (Devarim 17:19). This teaches that the fear is only learned by uninterrupted study.

Note that the verse says: "so that he will learn to fear" and not "so that he will fear". Because since this fear is not attained naturally. On the contrary, it is kept far from him due to the corporeality of his senses. Thus, it can only be acquired through learning, and the only manner in which one may learn to fear is through great diligence in the study of the Torah and its ways without interruption. Namely, through contemplating and examining this matter always, when he sits and when he walks, when he lies down and when he rises, until the truth of the matter becomes implanted in his mind, that is, the truth that His Divine presence (Shechina) is present everywhere, and of our actually (mamash) standing before Him at all times, every moment. Then he will fear G-d in truth.

This is what king David prayed for saying: "teach me Your way, O L-rd; I shall walk in Your truth. Unify my heart to fear Your Name"(Tehilim 86:11)

Messilat Yesharim

Chapter 26

The matter of holiness is dual. Its beginning is service [of G-d] while its end is reward; its beginning is exertion while its end is a [divine] gift. That is, its beginning is that which a man sanctifies himself, while its end is his being sanctified. This is what our sages, of blessed memory, said: "if a man sanctifies himself a little, he becomes much sanctified. If he sanctifies himself below, he becomes sanctified from above" (Yomah 39a).

The exertion is that which a man completely detaches and removes himself from the physical, and clings always, at all periods and times to his G-d. In this manner, the prophets were called "angels", as said of Aharon: "For a priest's lips shall guard knowledge, and Torah shall be sought from his mouth; for he is an angel of the L-rd of Hosts" (Malachi 2:7), and it is said: "but they mocked the angels (prophets) of G-d" (Divrei Hayamim II 36:16). Even when he is engaged in physical actions required for his bodily side, his soul will not budge from its clinging on high. This is as written: "my soul clings after You; Your right hand supports me"(Tehilim 63:9).

However, it is impossible for a man to place himself in such a state. For it is beyond his ability. He is after all a physical creature, of flesh and blood. Thus, I said that the end of Holiness is a gift. For that which is in man's ability to do is the initial exertion, pursuing true knowledge and continual thought on the sanctification of deed.

But the end is that the Holy One, blessed be He, will guide him on this path he desires to follow and imbue His holiness upon him, and sanctify him. Then this matter will succeed and he will be able to achieve this clinging with the blessed G-d constantly.

For that which his nature hinders this, the blessed G-d will help him and give him assistance. This is as the verse states: "G-d will not withhold good from those who walk wholeheartedly" (Tehilim 84:12).

Therefore, our sages said in the statement I brought: "a man sanctifies himself a little", which refers to that which a man can acquire through his own exertion. Then "he is sanctified much", which refers to the divine help which the Creator, blessed be He, aids him as I wrote.

Behold, for the man sanctified with the holiness of his Creator, even his physical deeds become actual matters of holiness. A sign of this is in "the eating of temple offerings", which our sages of blessed memory said: "the priests eat and the owners obtain atonement" (Pesachim 59b).

You can now see the difference between the Pure man and the Holy man. The physical actions of the pure man are only to him as necessity. His only intent in doing them is on their necessary aspect. Through this, his actions escape the evil side of the physical and remain pure. But they do not enter the domain of Holiness, for if it were possible to do without them, it would already have been better for him.

But for the Holy man who constantly clings to his G-d, whose soul treads freely among true thoughts in love of his Creator and fear of Him, behold, it is considered as if he is walking before G-d in the Land of the Living, while still here in this world.

Such a man is himself considered as a tabernacle, a temple and an altar. This is as our sages said (Gen. Rabba 62:6): "'and G-d went up from him' (Gen.35:13) - the forefathers are the divine chariot". Likewise, they said: "the righteous are the divine chariot".

For the Shechina (divine presence) dwells within them just as it dwelled in the Temple. Due to this, the food they eat is like a sacrifice offered upon the fire of the altar, for certainly it was a great elevation for those things to be offered on the altar, since they were offered before the Shechina.

The elevation was to such an extent that its kind, all over the world, was blessed, as our sages stated in a Midrash.

So too, the food and drink which the holy man eats elevates that food or drink as if it had actually been offered on the altar. This is similar to what our sages, of blessed memory, said: "one who brings a gift to a Torah scholar is as if he had offered first-fruits (Bikurim)" (Ketuvot 105b), and "[if a man wishes to offer a wine libation upon the altar], let him fill the throat of the Torah scholars with wine" (Yomah 71a).

This does not mean that Torah scholars were craving for food and drink, G-d forbid, that one fills their throats like one stuffs a glutton. Rather, the matter is according to the intent I explained. That Torah scholars who are holy in their ways and in all their deeds are actually just like the Temple and the altar, for the Shechina (divine presence) literally dwells upon them as it did in the Temple. Thus, what is offered to them is as offered on the altar, and the filling of their throat is as the filling of the basins.

In this way was all use they made of the things of this world. Since they were clinging to G-d's holiness, blessed be He, behold, it was an elevation and an enhancement for that thing which merited to be of use to a Tzadik (righteous person). Our sages already referred to the matter of the "stones at the place" which Yaakov took and put under his head: "Rabbi Yitzchak said: This tells us that all the stones gathered themselves together into one place and each one said: 'Upon me shall the righteous man rest his head'" (Chulin 91b).

The general principle of the matter: Holiness consists of one's clinging so much to his G-d that for any action he does, he will not separate nor budge from G-d, blessed be He, so that the physical things he uses will attain greater elevation than that which he diminishes in his clinging and level due to his using physical things.

However, this refers only to one whose mind and intellect is always fixed on G-d's greatness, blessed be He, and His exalted holiness, such that it is as if he is actually among the lofty angels while still in this world.

I already mentioned that a man is unable to do this on his own. He can only rouse himself in the matter and strive towards it. And this is after he has already acquired all of the previous virtuous traits we mentioned, from the beginning of Watchfulness until the Fear of Sin. Only with this will he approach the Holy and succeed. For if he lacks the previous traits, he will be like an outsider or a blemished [Kohen] of which it is stated: "an outsider (non-Kohen) shall not come near" (Bamidbar 18:4).

But if after he has prepared himself with all these preparations, he persistently clings with powerful love and intense fear in pondering G-d's greatness and infinite exaltedness, he will separate himself from physical matters little by little and will direct his heart in all his actions and movements to the true inner clinging, until, a spirit from on high will pour upon him and the Creator will cause His Name to rest upon him, as He does with all of His holy ones.

He will then actually be like an angel of G-d, and all his actions, even the lowly and the physical ones, will be like Temple sacrifices and services.

Behold, you can see that the way to acquire this trait is through much Separation, intense study of the secrets of divine providence, the hidden matters of the creation, and knowledge of His exaltedness, blessed be He, and His praises, until one clings greatly to Him, and knows how to have intent in his thoughts, as was proper for the Kohen to have intents while slaughtering the offering, receiving its blood, and sprinkling it, until he would draw down the blessing from G-d of life and peace.

Without this, it is impossible for him to reach this level, and he will remain physical and corporeal like all other human beings.

That which helps to attain this trait is much solitude and Separation, so that in the absence of distractions, one's soul will be able to strengthen more and cling to its Creator.

The detriments to this trait [of Holiness] are lack of true knowledge and much association with other people. For the physical meets its kind, awakens and strengthens, and the soul remains trapped in it and will not escape its prison.

But when one separates himself from others, remaining in solitude, and preparing himself for the receiving of His holiness, behold, in the way he wishes to go, he will be led, and with the divine help G-d will give him, his soul will strengthen within him and defeat the corporeal, cling to His holiness, blessed be He, and be rendered whole (perfect) through Him.

From there, he may ascend to a higher level, namely, Holy Spirit (Ruach HaKodesh), then his thinking will ascend beyond the bounds of human limits.

His clinging may reach such high levels that the key to revival of the dead will be given to him, as it was given to Eliyahu and Elisha. This will reveal how intensely is his clinging to G-d, blessed be He. For in His being the source of life, who bestows life to all living things, as our sages of blessed memory, said: "three keys the Holy One, blessed be He, has retained in His own hands and not entrusted into the hand of any emissary (angel): the Key of the Revival of the Dead..." (Taanit 2a). Behold, one who clings to the blessed G-d completely will be able to draw down even the flow of life itself from Him, which is, what is attributed to G-d more than anything else as I wrote. This is what the Beraitha concludes: "Holiness brings to the Holy Spirit, and the Holy Spirit brings to the Revival of the Dead".

I know, dear reader, that you realize just as I do, that I have not completed in this book all the principles of piety, nor did I say all there is to say on this area. For it has no end and its study is without limit.

But I spoke a bit on each of the particulars of the Beraitha which I based this book on. This may serve as a start and beginning to expand study in these matters. For their ways have been revealed and their paths opened to our eyes so that we may walk in them on the straight path. On such matters it is written: "Let the wise man hear and increase learning. The understanding man shall acquire wise counsels" (Mishlei 1:5), and "if one comes to purify himself, he is helped" (Shabbat 104a), and "for the L-rd gives wisdom; from His mouth comes knowledge and understanding" (Mishlei 2:6), so that every man may straighten his ways before his Creator.

It is evident, that each individual needs correction and guidance according to his particular trade and occupation. For the way of Piety appropriate for one whose occupation is Torah study is not the way of Piety for one who needs to hire himself out to work for his fellow. Nor are these two the way of Piety appropriate for one occupied in business. Similarly, for all other various affairs of human beings in the world. Each person according to who he is, will be the ways of piety suitable for him. This is not because Piety varies, for it is certainly equal for everyone, since piety is nothing more than doing what is pleasing to one's Maker.

But since the subjects vary, it is impossible for the means which bring to this goal to not vary accordingly with each individual. Thus, one can be a complete Chasid if he is a man whose mouth does not interrupt from Torah study, just like one who, due to necessity, is a lowly laborer. And it is written: "G-d has made everything for His sake" (Mishlei 16:4), and "in all your ways know Him, and He will straighten your paths" (Mishlei 3:6).

May the blessed G-d, in His mercy, open our eyes in His Torah, teach us His ways, guide us in His paths, so that we may merit to give honor to His Name and bring gratification to Him. "The glory of G-d will be forever; G-d will rejoice with His works" (Tehilim 104:21), "Israel will rejoice with its Maker; the children of Zion will exult with their King" (Tehilim 149:2), amen, amen, amen!

Messulat Chapter 26 Yesharim

www.ingramcontent.com/pod-product-compliance
Lightning Source LLC
Chambersburg PA
CBHW070132080526
44586CB00015B/1653